BROWNING STUDIES

BY

VERNON C. HARRINGTON

ASSISTANT PROFESSOR OF ENGLISH IN MIDDLEBURY
COLLEGE

ARTI et VERITATI

BOSTON: RICHARD G. BADGER
TORONTO: THE COPP CLARK CO., LIMITED
MCMXV

THE GORHAM PRESS, BOSTON, U.S.A.

Dedication

TO

THE STUDENTS

WHO HAVE STUDIED BROWNING WITH ME
IN OBERLIN AND MIDDLEBURY

You must not mind if I dedicate these Studies to you, for most of them were prepared for you and your interest (may I venture to say enthusiasm?) in them is responsible for their publication. Peradventure, if your eyes light on this book, its words may bring to your minds the course in Nineteenth Century Poetry, the gray classroom, and those long and forbidding lists of questions for written tests, to be answered without regard to floods of sunshine or of rain outside the windows. I hope this book may also bring keenly to your thoughts the good friends you found among the English Poets of the nineteenth century and, above all, the imperial soul of Robert Browning. You may be sure that working over these lectures, to revise them somewhat and to get them written out so that some one besides myself can understand the abbreviations, has brought you all many times before my mind's eye and has made more plain to me the eager and generous spirit which so many of you showed and has caused me to realize anew how your spirit helped me to put into orderly presentation something of what has come out of the years of my reading of Browning. And so I dedicate to you now these lectures, because, in a very real sense, they already belong to you.

PREFACE

THESE Browning Studies were given in Oberlin College, in the Department of English in the course on Nineteenth Century Poetry, in the second semester of the year 1908–09, and were repeated in the corresponding semester of the year 1909–10. They constituted a course in the Summer Session of Middlebury College in 1913, and were given here again as a part of the study of Nineteenth Century Poetry in the second semester of the year 1913–14. It should be explained also that the greater part of the study of *The Ring and the Book* was written before those Oberlin days, and that since those days *Bishop Blougram's Apology*, *A Death in the Desert*, and *Reverie* have been added to the list of poems taken up; also that, besides being used in connection with the college classes mentioned above, several of the lectures have been given in various places.

The interest taken by the students in these studies has suggested their publication. They are now printed as given in the classroom, with some revision. Abbreviations are written out more than in the author's notes, but no attempt has been made to reproduce the extemporaneous elaboration and explanation given in the classroom. Lectures which occupied several classroom hours are here sometimes combined into a single chapter.

These studies do not pretend to be exhaustive. They are simply an introduction to some of Browning's best work. They are intended now, as they were in the classroom, for those who have not read Browning at all before, or very little. The idea which people get, that they cannot understand Browning, is one of those "literary superstitions" which are passed from one to another. I remember well my pleasure when I first seriously tried to read Browning and found that I could do it. A part of the pleasure of teaching Browning, in the courses already referred to, was enjoying the surprise of students, when they found they could read Browning and get something out of him. It is true, however, that in reading Browning a great deal depends on what sort of a start we get, *i.e.* what poems we read first. I do not wonder at the experience of the Cincinnati gentleman (referred to in Chapter II) who began with *Red Cotton Night-Cap Country*. These studies for the classroom were planned with purpose that students might begin Browning right, as far as I could understand from my own experience what is the right way to begin, and, for the same reason, they are now given in printed form in the same order.

I confess that I owe Robert Browning a debt which I can never pay, for it is hardly an exaggeration to say that Browning opened a new world to me. His optimism and his red-blooded joy in the intensity of struggle in the present hour and his stern facing of life have done me an immense good. The optimism of most people makes me more pessimistic and makes the whole situation seem hopeless, because most people's optimism is of a childish sort, due to their good digestion and agreeable experiences and to their ignorance of the evil in the world and their blindness to the beauty and the cruelty of human life. But Robert Browning's optimism is not that of a child, but of a fullgrown man who realizes keenly the worst there is in the world, and yet, in the face of it all, believes in the existence of and the triumph of good. I hold that no man who has found a good thing should keep it for himself alone. Therefore, if Browning has been good for me and if I can encourage some one else to get acquainted with him, it is my duty and privilege to do so.

A practical suggestion may not be amiss as to a way of using the present book. It should be used never apart from but only alongside a good edition of Browning. It will be well to read the introductory lectures first; then to take up the poems designated in the studies that follow, each poem in turn, reading the matter given in the lecture, then reading the poem, then referring again to the lecture and again to the poem as long as the lecture can be found of any assistance. I shall be glad if the notes and comments I have written down can be of service in some such way as this, but always the poem is the thing.

V. C. H.

Middlebury, Vermont,
    December 12, 1914.

CONTENTS

BROWNING STUDIES

I

AN INTRODUCTION TO THE STUDY OF ROBERT BROWNING

In all the world there is no place with greater store of associations than Westminster Abbey. It is crowded with graves. It seems almost like a vast tomb, instead of a church. Here in dust lie so many great and renowned. Where else can you find so many and famous names as along the walls and on the floor of Westminster Abbey?

And there is no place where the vanity of human life comes in upon your spirit so. In the gloom of that church, one feels very keenly the truth of St. James' words: "For what is your life? It is even a vapour, that appeareth for a little time, and then vanisheth away." Each time I visited Westminster Abbey, it had the same effect. It is a curious feeling to stand on the stones which cover the graves of those whose names and greatness have been familiar to us from childhood up. Mouths stopped with dust, strong hands disintegrated, brave hearts the helpless prey of corruption, and mighty brain of one after another turned into a handful of earth! "After life's fitful fever," they "sleep well." I know one day I left the church and went out into the cloisters, and walked while the winter sun went down, — and the nothingness of human life, the pitifulness and absurdity of all our struggle, filled the hori-zon of my thoughts. Such desolate words as the Psalmists

wrote would keep coming into mind with fresh meaning:
"We spend our years as a tale that is told." "As for man,
his days are as grass; as a flower of the field, so he flour-
isheth. For the wind passeth over it, and it is gone, and
the place thereof shall know it no more."

And in Westminster Abbey, I always paused a long time
by two graves among the others so crowded in the Poets'
Corner. There they lie, side by side, each under a plain
slab in the floor,[1] Alfred Tennyson and Robert Browning.
As they lived, the two lights which outshone all their con-
temporaries, so they lie there now, — side by side.

There is at once a temptation to compare these two men,
and partisan admirers are constantly praising one and dis-
paraging the other. This is quite unnecessary. They are
very different. There is room for both. Each supple-
ments the other. Each has his mission and makes his
contribution. We defraud ourselves, if we choose either
Tennyson or Browning and neglect the other. How these
two men felt toward each other may be judged from these
two dedications:

(1) Browning's volume of *Selections*, 1872, selected from
his works and arranged by himself, with Preface, and

> "Dedicated to
> Alfred Tennyson
> in poetry — illustrious and consummate
> in friendship — noble and sincere."

(2) Tennyson's volume *Tiresias and Other Poems*, 1885,

> "To my good friend
> Robert Browning
> whose genius and geniality
> will best appreciate what may be best
> and make most allowance for what may be worst."

[1] A bust of Tennyson stands not far off.

Nothing could show mutual appreciation and admiration better than these dedications. Then, let not the admirers of either Tennyson or Browning do an injustice to the other.

We have given some weeks to the study of Tennyson. We come now to the study of Robert Browning. After many years of familiarity with Browning's poems, it is with a certain sense of reverence that I turn to them now. "I was not ever thus." In college, I sneered and jeered at Robert Browning. I repeated all the threadbare jokes about the obscurity of his style and nobody's knowing what he meant. I argued that enthusiasm for Browning was a fad and was pretended by men and women who couldn't understand Browning. In all these remarks, in which my college mates usually acquiesced, I thought I was smart. But the fact is that it was all because *I didn't know any better*. That is my only excuse. The day came when I read a statement of Browning's own,[1] that he had never been wilfully obscure, that, if people couldn't understand his poems, he was sorry, for he had tried to say what he meant. It occurred to me that the difficulty in understanding Browning might be one of those "literary superstitions"[2] which get afloat in the world, and I waded into the study of Browning for myself. I found a mine of wealth and beauty. I found a man who faces life unflinchingly,

[1] This statement of Browning's I am not now able to locate. I give it in effect, and I remember it pretty well and especially the impression it made on me. The nearest I find is a statement in a letter written in 1868 to W. G. Kingsland, quoted by Griffin and Minchin, *Life of Robert Browning*, p. 302, where Browning says: "But I never designedly tried to puzzle people, as some of my critics have supposed."

[2] In those days, I did not know this fortunate phrase by which to call such things. The phrase is one of the Rev. A. J. Carlyle's, Fellow of University College, Oxford, and Vicar of St. Martin's and All Saints', in his lectures on Some Common Characteristics of Mediæval Literatures.

whose comprehensive sympathy has wrestled with more of life's problems than anyone in English Literature except Shakespeare. After some years of putting him to the test, often in the night and the storm, I can only say in bluntest simplest manner, *Robert Browning has helped me live*. I am not the only one — I have seen it in many others. Better acquaintance with Browning has won to his side many who opposed or laughed at him. A friend of mine told me that in his class in Princeton some of the men who seemed most unlikely to do so became enthusiastic for Browning in taking a course in which his works were studied. It seldom fails that the fondness for Browning grows with the years of acquaintance. He wears well. I am not a blind partisan of Browning. I see his defects. But I know also the soul-satisfying quality of his thoughts. Robert Browning will bring something into the life of anyone who sincerely studies his poems. When things get thick, you will find Robert Browning standing by you. He has been through it, and has not flinched. The fact that there could be such a man as he was makes me believe more in humanity. And the words which he has penned have been to many almost like food and drink in the desert.

This confession I make for your sakes. Let me ask you, then, to put away your prejudices and to reserve your judgment until we are done with these weeks of Browning study, lest you be found pronouncing judgment on yourselves, as I did in my college days.

I. ABOUT THE BOOKS

1. Of Browning's Works, as far as one-volume editions are concerned, the *Globe Edition*, edited by Augustine Birrell, New York, The Macmillan Co., is the best. No one-volume edition of Browning can be altogether satis-

factory, there is so much matter to put in. The Globe Edition was formerly (1896–1907) published in two volumes, but by the use of thinner paper, from 1907 on, it has been put into one volume, of something over 1300 pages. This was the edition used by the students to whom these lectures were delivered, and therefore the references in these lectures are to the pages and lines of this edition.

2. A good edition is the *Camberwell Browning*, with introductions and notes by Miss Charlotte Porter and Miss Helen A. Clarke, 12 vols., New York, T. Y. Crowell & Co., 1898.[1] The volumes are sold separately as well as in sets, and, on this account, the numbers are in small Arabic numerals at the bottom of the back. The notes are a great assistance, but unfortunately are not always accurate, and sometimes provoke dissent.[2] This edition may be had also with Miss Porter and Miss Clarke's *Browning Study Programmes*, two vols. uniform with the others, making 14 vols. in all.

3. The best biography of Browning is *The Life of Robert Browning, with Notices of his Writings, his Family, and his Friends*, by W. Hall Griffin, completed and edited by Harry Christopher Minchin, New York, The Macmillan Co., 1910. This is done with great care and thoroughness.

4. Any mention of important books for Browning study should include Edmund Gosse's *Robert Browning: Personalia*, Boston, Houghton, Mifflin & Co., 1890. These *Personalia* are from notes supplied by Robert Browning himself.

5. Mrs. Sutherland Orr's *Life and Letters of Robert*

---

[1] This is the same as the *Arno Edition* which was published by Geo. D. Sproul, New York, 1899, (no longer issued).

[2] For a case in which we are obliged to dissent, see our note on the word "lathen," Appendix C of the present volume.

Browning, published in two vols., 1891, (and in a one-vol. edition the same year), has been esteemed an indispensable source of information, and so it is. The author of it, Mrs. Alexandra Leighton Orr, became an intimate friend of the Brownings, and had in hand much unusual material for a biography. But, because of haste and inaccuracy, the biography proved unsatisfactory to the poet's son and other relatives.[1] There has been issued, however, a new and enlarged edition, revised by Frederic G. Kenyon, one vol., Boston, Houghton, Mifflin & Co., 1908.

6. Mrs. Orr's *Handbook to the Works of Robert Browning*, published in 1885, is now in its eleventh edition and is very good. This Handbook was approved by Robert Browning himself, and his son's attitude toward it, in the same conversation with Prof. Phelps referred to in our footnote, confirms that approval. It is published by Geo. Bell & Sons of London; The Macmillan Co., New York.

7. A very useful and reliable book is George Willis Cooke's *Guide-Book to the Poetic and Dramatic Works of Robert Browning*, Boston, Houghton, Mifflin & Co., 1891. It will commend itself to anyone who refers to its pages to any extent.

8. One of the most valuable books for general reference is *The Browning Cyclopædia* by Edward Berdoe, 1st edition 1891, 7th edition 1912, London, George Allen & Co. Ltd.; New York, The Macmillan Co. This book is sometimes disappointing. Dr. Berdoe cannot avoid reading into Browning too much of his own Roman Catholic faith and his zeal against vivisection and such methods of re-

---

[1] See article by Prof. Wm. Lyon Phelps, *Robert Browning as Seen by his Son*, in the *Century Magazine*, Jan., 1913, (vol. LXXXV, no. 3), pp. 417–420 — especially Mr. Barrett Browning's remarks about this biography, on p. 418.

search.[1] But the book is a vast collection of information on Browning's writings and things referred to by Browning, and is an exceedingly handy "business book" for Browning study.

9. A list of some of the other editions now in print of Browning's works, and of books about Browning, which would naturally stand here, has been transferred to the end of the present volume of lectures. For further details in this line, the reader is therefore referred to Appendix A. We have no desire to bury up Browning in books about him. Browning's own words are the main thing, and any books about him and his writings are useful only as they send readers to his own words with greater eagerness and better understanding. It is a pitiful thing to be always reading "about it and about" and miss the thing itself. The placing of the list at the end of the volume instead of at this point does not, however, at all imply that books there mentioned fall short in value or in ability to lead the reader to Browning himself, but only that it is better that such a list should stand there. The list, although at the end of the book, is in the reader's hands, to be referred to at any time.

II. Dates outlining Browning's Life

The following dates [2] will serve as a sort of outline of Browning's life:

[1] Cf. his attempt (7th ed., p. 105) to interpret a part of *Childe Roland* in some such way.   Browning was against vivisection, but he was not arguing against anything of the sort in *Childe Roland*.

[2] The dates have been checked up by Griffin-and Minchin's *Life of Robert Browning*.   In revising the present lecture I have depended on the same biography also for accurate details.   So many accounts of Browning's life are vague and deal so much in misleading generalities that it is an unalloyed pleasure to real the careful and painstaking work of Griffin and Michin.

1. 1812, May 7, Robert Browning was born, in Camberwell, a suburb of London on its southern side. His sister
Sarah Anna [1] was born Jan. 7, 1814. These were the
only children in the family. The house in which they were
born stood in Southampton St., near Dowlas Common
which came to be called Cottage Green and is now built
up although the name Cottage Green remains. While
Sarah Anna was still an infant, the family moved into
another house on the same street, and about 1824 they
moved from that house to Hanover Cottage, also in Southampton St., and this they occupied for 16 years.

2. 1820–26 (or 1821–26), from the time when he was
eight or nine years old until he was fourteen, the boy
attended the Rev. Thomas Ready's school, in Peckham
about a mile from home.

3. 1828, Oct., Browning began study in London University.[2] He was then 16 years old. His name was
entered under date of June 30, 1828, but classes did not
begin until the Fall Term. The studies were Greek,
Latin, and German. He continued for one term, but left
abruptly during the second term, some time after Christmas. This was his only college education.

4. 1829, in the spring, he decided on poetry for his life-work.

---

[1] Her name stands Sarah Anna written by her father's hand in the family
Bible (record copied by Griffin and Minchin and printed at the beginning
of their *Life of Browning*), but the two names became later combined into
Sarianna.

[2] This institution from its inception in 1825 was known as London University, but received a charter in 1836 as *University College*. Hence the
confusion in references to Browning's studying there, — some saying he
studied at London University, some saying at University College, London.
It was called London University when Browning attended it. University
College, London, still continues on the original site. The fact that up to
1836 it was called London University should not confuse it with the present
University of London.

5. 1834, he travelled to St. Petersburg with Chevalier George de Benkhausen, the Russian Consul-General to England. Left London Saturday, Mch. 1, and was back in England in three months.

6. 1838, first [1] visit to Italy. Sailed on the afternoon of Friday, April 13, landed at Trieste May 30, and arrived at Venice Wednesday morning, June 1. Within the next three weeks he visited many of the cities in that part of Italy, and returned to Venice. Then went to Verona, and journeyed home by way of the Tyrol and the Rhine.

7. 1840, Dec., the Browning family left Camberwell and moved to Hatcham, another suburb. The poet made his home with his parents until his marriage.

8. 1844, his second Italian journey, leaving England in the summer and returning in December.

9. 1845, May 20, Robert Browning first met Elizabeth Barrett. She had received her first letter from him on Jan. 10, 1845, but it was some months before he could see her.

10. 1846, Sept. 12, Saturday, about noon or a little before, Robert Browning and Elizabeth Barrett were married at St. Marylebone Church, London. It was a secret marriage, her two sisters knowing it, but her father not knowing. The only witnesses were Miss Barrett's maid and Browning's cousin James Silverthorne.

11. 1846, Sept. 19, Saturday afternoon (just a week later), she stole out of her father's house, No. 50 Wimpole St., London, with her maid and her spaniel, Flush, went around the corner to Hodgson's bookstore in Great Marylebone St. and met Robert Browning. They took the 5 : 00

---

[1] "This was Browning's first Italian visit; he did *not*, as has been repeatedly stated, visit Italy in 1834." — Griffin and Minchin, *Life*, pp. 94, 95, footnote.

P.M. train for Southampton, and so to Paris and from there to Italy. Her father never forgave her and never saw her again.

12. 1846–47, they spent the winter in Pisa.

13. 1847, April, they came to Florence. At first they took furnished apartments in the Via delle Belle Donne, close to the Piazza Santa Maria Novella. That summer, leaving those apartments to seek cooler quarters, they took a suite of rooms up one flight of stairs [1] in the Casa Guidi,[2] south of the Arno, at the corner of the Via Maggio and the Via Mazetta, almost opposite the Pitti Palace. In October, they moved to other furnished rooms in the Piazza Pitti, to get more sunlight for the winter.

14. 1848, May, they leased the flat in the Casa Guidi which they had occupied the summer before, — seven rooms, the favorite suite of the last Count Guidi. They took the rooms unfurnished, paying an annual rental of 25 guineas (between $125 and $130). This was their home. They often travelled and sometimes rented their flat furnished, in their absence, but returned here when they came "home."

15. 1848, summer, they travelled on the east side of Italy, visiting Fano, Ancona, Rimini, and Ravenna.

16. 1849, Mch. 9, their son, Robert Wiedemann Barrett Browning,[3] was born in the Casa Guidi. He was their only child.

17. 1849, Robert Browning's mother died this year,

---

[1] The rooms are on what in Europe is called the first floor, *i.e.* the floor up one flight, not the street floor. In America, we usually call that the second floor.

[2] So named from the fact that it was formerly the residence of the Counts Guidi. Casa signifies "house," or "home."

[3] Usually spoken of, in later years, as Mr. R. Barrett Browning, or Mr. Barrett Browning.

at the home of the family in Hatcham. Her death occurred soon after the poet's son was born.

18. 1849, July–Oct., Browning and his wife and their boy spent the summer at the Baths of Lucca. There are three villages in the narrow valley, — the lowest called Ponte, the next Alla Villa, and the third Bagni Caldi. The Brownings occupied a house in the third and highest village.

19. 1851, after nearly five years' absence, they came to London, stopping a month in Venice, and stopping also at Padua and Milan, crossing the Alps by coach over the St. Gotthard Pass, and spending several weeks in Paris. They arrived in London late in July, and started back to Paris Sept. 25.

20. 1851–52, they spent the winter in Paris. In Nov. the poet's father and sister visited them there. In April the lease which his father had on the house at Hatcham expired, and he and his daughter settled in Paris that spring. This was their permanent residence from that time till the father's death.

21. 1852, end of June, the poet and his wife and son returned to London and spent the summer there, and set out for Italy again early in Nov. They arrived at the Casa Guidi in Florence after an absence of 16 months.

22. 1853, summer, again at the Baths of Lucca, this time in the middle village, Alla Villa. Returned to Florence in Oct., but stayed only a short time.

23. 1853–54, their first winter in Rome. Returned to Florence near the end of May, 1854.

24. 1855, they returned to London, arriving there the second week in June. From there they went to Paris in October.

25. 1855–56, winter spent in Paris.

26. 1856, near the end of June, they went back to England again, and spent the summer in London, and at Ventnor and West Cowes, on the Isle of Wight, — starting back to Italy from London in October.

27. 1856–57, winter in Florence. In April, 1857, Mrs. Browning's father died in London.

28. 1857, July–Oct., spent again at Alla Villa, the middle village of the Baths of Lucca.

29. 1857–58, another winter in Florence.

30. 1858, in the spring, started for France, arriving in Paris on the birthday of the poet's father. Stayed two weeks in Paris, and then they all (Browning and his family, and his father and his sister) went to Normandy and stayed eight weeks by the seaside in the outskirts of Havre. Returned to Paris for four weeks more. Then started for Italy Oct. 12. Stayed only a month in Florence.

31. 1858–59, wintered in Rome. The winter climate of Rome was found to be better for Mrs. Browning's health than the winter climate of Florence. So three consecutive winters were spent in Rome.

32. 1859, May, returned to Florence. August, went to Siena for the rest of the summer; lived in the Villa Alberti at Marciano, two miles out of the city. Left there in the autumn and stopped briefly in Florence.

33. 1859–60, winter in Rome.

34. 1860, summer was spent at the same house occupied the preceding summer, near Siena. Returned to Rome in Sept.

35. 1860–61, winter in Rome.

36. 1861, spring, Mrs. Browning, whose health had been growing more frail for several years, had a sharp and alarming attack and it seemed as if she would strangle. But she recovered sufficiently to travel to Florence. They

arrived in Florence June 6. The last stage of her illness began on June 23, but she was not confined to her room until the 28th. Even then she thought she was better in the evening.

37. 1861, June 29, about four o'clock in the morning, Mrs. Browning died, in the Casa Guidi. There is a tablet on the house, placed there by the municipality of Florence, with an inscription by the Italian poet and patriot Tommaseo :[1]

> "Here wrote and died Elizabeth Barrett Browning, who . . . made of her verse a golden link between Italy and England."

38. 1861, Aug., Browning came to Paris with his son. He never saw Florence again. That summer he spent some weeks, his father and sister with him, at St. Enoget. He came with his boy to London in October. After some months, he leased a house, No. 19 Warwick Crescent, — at first temporarily, but it proved satisfactory and he kept it. This was his home for the next 25 years.

39. 1862, spring, he was offered the editorship of the *Cornhill Magazine*, but declined it.

40. 1862, summer at Cambo and Biarritz in France.

41. 1865, he visited Oxford to see Benjamin Jowett, Senior Tutor (afterwards Master) of Balliol, with a view to putting his son in College. Jowett's friendship meant much to Browning in the years that followed.

42. 1866, his father died in Paris, and Robert Browning took his sister Sarianna to London to make her home with him. She never married. They were constant companions from that time.

---

[1] The inscription is in Italian on the tablet, complete as follows : "Qui scrisse e morì Elizabetta Barrett Browning, che in cuore di donna conciliava scienza di dotto e spirito di poeta, e fece del suo verso aureo anello fra Italia e Inghilterra. Pone questa lapide Firenze grata 1861."

43. 1866, summer, spent at Croisic in Brittany, as was also the summer of the year following. Several other summers were spent in Brittany (those of 1869 and '70 were at St. Aubin). On their summer holidays 1873–77, in France and Switzerland, Miss Anne Egerton Smith was with the Brownings.

44. 1867, Browning received from the University of Oxford the degree of M.A. The same year he was made Honorary Fellow of Balliol College.

45. 1868, he was offered the position of Lord Rector [1] of St. Andrews University, but declined it.

46. 1875, the Lord Rectorship of the University of Glasgow was offered to him, but he declined it. He declined it again in 1884.

47. 1878, Browning visited Venice and Asolo again, breaking the journey at the Splügen Pass. He had not seen Italy for 17 years. He had not been in Asolo for 40 years. From 1878 on, his autumns were usually spent in north Italy, stopping somewhere on the way in the Alps during five or six of the warmer weeks preceding. Only three autumns was he prevented by circumstances from going to Italy — 1882, 1884, and 1886. He did not go further south than Venice. Venice held him by strong affection.

48. 1879, he received the degree of LL.D. from Cambridge University.

49. 1881, the Browning Society of London was founded. The chief movers were Dr. F. J. Furnivall and Miss Emily Hickey. There were soon branches in many parts of the United Kingdom. The forming of this Society was a great compliment to Robert Browning, and its discussions and publications increased materially the sale of his works.

[1] *i.e.* President of the University, to use the title which goes with the similar office in the majority of American universities.

50. 1882, Browning received the degree of D.C.L. from Oxford University.

51. 1884, he received the degree of LL.D. from the University of Edinburgh.

52. 1885, Browning's son went with him and his sister to Venice. He had not been there since he was a child. The idea of buying a palace in Venice took hold upon Browning and his son on this visit, and a purchase was almost concluded, but came to naught.

53. 1887, June, Browning gave up the house on Warwick Crescent, London, which had been his home for so many years, and took a better and roomier house in De Vere Gardens.

54. 1887, Oct., his son married Fannie Coddington, of New York.

55. 1888, Aug., on his way to Venice this year, Browning's stop was at Primiero in the Dolomite Alps. His son had bought the Rezzonico Palace (Palazzo Rezzonico) on the Grand Canal, although he had not yet moved in. But this was a special inducement to Browning to make the journey to Venice, and he stayed there unusually long.

56. 1889, Feb., he was again in London.

57. 1889, summer, Browning visited all his favorite haunts in England, not knowing that it was his last visit.

58. 1889, that summer, Mrs. Arthur Bronson, an American lady in whose house in Venice Browning and his sister had stayed so many times, urged them to come and visit her in Asolo. She had there a house, "La Mura," which was niched in one of the towers of the city wall and which she occupied when the weather was hot in Venice. To Asolo, then, on their way to Venice, the poet and his sister came, toward the end of the summer, and here they spent a number of weeks.

59. 1889, Nov. 1, Browning and his sister arrived at his son's house in Venice. Late in November, after his usual walk, it was noticed that Browning had a cold. He never would take much care of himself.[1] The cold developed into bronchitis and on Dec. 1 his son's physician was called. The bronchitis grew better, but symptoms developed, threatening heart-failure. On the evening of Dec. 12, he himself was aware that the end was near.

60. 1889, Dec. 12, Thursday, at 10:00 P.M., Robert Browning died without pain, in the Palazzo Rezzonico, his son's house in Venice. Upon this house the city of Venice has placed a tablet to Robert Browning, which contains two lines of his own:[2]

> "Open my heart and you will see
> Graved inside of it, 'Italy.'"

61. 1889, Dec. 15, Sunday, a private funeral service was held in the house, and then the body was taken, as the Venetian law requires, to the mortuary island San Michele and placed in the chapel there. The ceremony of transferring the body to this place was very impressive, — a great flotilla of gondolas following the funeral barge.

62. 1889, Dec. 31, Robert Browning was buried in Westminster Abbey.

[1] Cf. what Barrett Browning said to Prof. Phelps of his father's last illness in the article in the *Century Magazine*, Jan., 1913, already referred to.

[2] The inscription reads:

A
ROBERTO BROWNING
MORTO IN QUESTO PALAZZO
IL 12 DICEMBRE 1889
VENEZIA
POSE

The lines from Browning are below toward the right hand corner. They are from "*De Gustibus* —" Browning's Works, Globe Ed., p. 239, ll. 17, 18. It may be necessary to repeat that, throughout these lectures, the references to Browning's works are made to the Globe Edition, 1 vol., New York, 1907.

III. A More Connected Account of Browning's Life

Within the framework of these bare dates took place the earthly experience of the man who wrote at the age of twenty: [1]

"I am made up of an intensest life."

That intensity of life increased rather than diminished, as the years went by. As Stopford Brooke [2] well says: "It was a life lived fully, kindly, lovingly, at its just height, from the beginning to the end."

1. Robert Browning's father, also named Robert Browning, held a position in the Bank of England. [3] He was born in 1782, in Battersea, a suburb lying on the bank of the Thames, southwest of London. He was, on his father's side, of an old English family, the Brownings of Dorsetshire and Wiltshire. His mother was a West Indian lady [4] who owned a large estate at St. Kitt's. She died when he was seven years old. He was sent to the West Indies at the age of twelve, on account of his father's second marriage, but, when he grew older, refused to stay on the plantation because of his hatred of slavery, and returned to England at the age of twenty, and presently secured a clerkship in the Bank. With his position in the Bank,

[1] In *Pauline*, p. 5, l. 3.

[2] Stopford A. Brooke, *The Poetry of Robert Browning*, New York, 1902, p. 441.

[3] He was connected with the Bank nearly 50 years, 1803–1852.

[4] Many accounts of Browning's life speak of his father's mother as a "creole." The word is avoided here simply because it is so misunderstood. The word creole correctly used does not at all imply that there is any admixture of African blood. It is properly applied to descendants of French or Spanish settlers in the vicinity of the Gulf of Mexico, as in Louisiana, Florida, or the West Indies.

c

he had money enough and time enough for intellectual development and the accumulation of a fine collection of books. He had immense vitality, unusual skill in drawing, great intellectual keenness, and wide and various learning. Something of the ideals and moral fiber of the man may be seen in the fact that, because he could not tolerate slavery, he sacrificed the plantation inherited from his mother, which would have yielded him wealth.

2. His wife, Sarah Anna [1] Wiedemann, the mother of Robert Browning the poet, was of mixed Scotch-German blood, — daughter of a Scotch mother and a German father, William Wiedemann, a shipowner at Dundee, who had come from Hamburg. She was born in Dundee, but she and her sister resided for some time with an uncle in Camberwell. She did not have the vigorous health which her husband had and, in the latter part of her life especially, suffered much from neuralgia. She was gentle, deeply religious,[2] and passionately fond of music.

3. We hear it said that "blood will tell." It told in the case of the poet Robert Browning. (*a*) From his father he received splendid health and almost inexhaustible vitality, intellectual eagerness and capacity, and a taste for art. (*b*) From his mother, a thoroughly German metaphysical turn of mind, a fondness for music and ability in music, and a deeply reverent and sometimes mystical attitude toward the things invisible and eternal.

---

[1] So stands the name in her husband's hand-writing in the family Bible :

"Robert Browning married to Sarah Anna Wiedemann at Camberwell Feb 19 1811."

(Griffin and Minchin, *Life*, p. 1).

Her name and her daughter's are usually written Sarianna.

[2] Browning's mother became a member of the Congregational Church in York St., Walworth, in 1806, and his father, though brought up in the Church of England, joined the Congregational Church in 1820.

4. One of Browning's earliest recollections is of himself sitting on his father's knee before the fire in the library, listening with rapt attention as his father told him the tale of the siege of Troy, while he heard his mother in the next room singing a low Gaelic lament. It would not be strange, if that boy should amount to something.

5. Camberwell, where the boy was born, though now really built up with London south of the Thames, was then a village, lying between the slopes of Denmark Hill, Herne Hill, and Champion Hill. Its church tower could be seen from the Thames bridges. Camberwell and its vicinity were well-known as a place of rural beauty,[1] — with bright fields, hedgerows, and fine trees. The two strains of interest which gave such equilibrium to Browning's life were both here at the beginning, — the world of Nature around him, the teeming city and the "world of men"[2] just at hand.

6. Robert Browning was chiefly a self-educated man. (*a*) The beginning of his education was found in the storehouse of his father's mind, and, as years went on, it was continued in his father's books. (*b*) He was sent to a day-school, taught by a woman near his home, but had to be removed because he was so much more proficient in reading and spelling than the other pupils were that it aroused the jealousy of their parents. (*c*) He was very fond of outdoor life and sports, and of all living things. In the course of the years, his pets included owls, monkeys, magpies, hedgehogs, an eagle, a toad, and two snakes.

[1] It is significant that a butterfly, the *Vanessa antiopa*, rare in England though common in central and southern Europe, was found in Camberwell so much more frequently than anywhere else that its common name is the Camberwell Beauty.

[2] Browning, *Parting at Morning*, p. 228, l. 30:

"And the need of a world of men for me."

(*d*) From the age of eight or nine until he was fourteen he attended, as a weekly boarder, a school conducted by the Rev. Thomas Ready and his sisters in Peckham. He was first taught and looked after by the Misses Ready, and, as he grew older, he was taught by Mr. Ready himself. It was a good school, as schools went in those days, but he was always impatient with the petty and mechanical teaching to which he was subjected, and got more from the days spent at home on the hill above the church or in the library with his father's books. When he was nearly thirty, passing Ready's school with Alfred Domett, he spoke of "the disgust [1] with which he always thought of the place," and fifty years after those schooldays he told Domett that "they taught him nothing there." (*e*) From the age of 14 onward, he went on with his studies at home, — two years with a tutor in French, two teachers in music (one for theory and the other for technique), much reading, and lessons in dancing, riding, boxing, and fencing. (*f*) His only other attendance at school was at London University in Gower St., in the founding of which his father was a shareholder, subscribing £100. The boy began there the fall after he was sixteen. It is usually said that his chief study was Greek. He continued less than two terms. This was the only college education he ever received, and with this his formal education stopped, although he attended, during the year following, some of Dr. Blundell's lectures at Guy's Hospital. (*g*) But though his formal education had ceased, he had just begun. All that vast education which makes him the most learned man that ever wrote English verse he accumulated for himself in the years that followed.

[1] Commenting on this remark, Griffin and Minchin explain that what disgusted him was the restraint put upon his imaginative faculties.

7. At the age of 17, in the spring following his college experience, Robert Browning deliberately looked life in the face and deliberately decided to make poetry his life-work. He went at once into his preparation for it, one of his first moves being to read and digest the whole of Dr. Samuel Johnson's Dictionary. Then he plunged into reading, at his home in Camberwell and especially in the British Museum.

8. His first published literary work was *Pauline*, written when he was 20 years old. The date at the end of the poem, Oct. 22, 1832, is the date of the conception of the plan of which *Pauline* is a part. On that evening he had seen Edmund Kean play in *Richard III* at Richmond. The date of the Introduction, London, January, 1833, is the date of the completion of this fragment, — the only part of the work ever written. No publisher would take the risk on it. His aunt, Mrs. James Silverthorne, furnished the money [1] to pay for its publication. It was published, without the author's name, by Saunders and Otley, London, 1833.

The poem is crude and amateurish but full of unusual promise. On the fly leaf of his own copy now in the Dyce and Forster Library at the South Kensington Museum, there is, in Browning's handwriting, this: "The following poem was written in pursuance of a foolish plan which occupied me mightily for a time, and which had for its object the enabling me to assume and realize I know not how many different characters. . . . Only this crab remains of the shapely Tree of Life in this Fool's Paradise of mine. — R. B." The poem was soon for-

---

[1] Mrs. Silverthorne was his mother's sister Christiana. Griffin and Minchin (p. 57) relate that she gave him £30 to defray the cost of publishing *Pauline;* the cost was £26 5s., and the rest was spent for advertising.

gotten,[1] and Dante Gabriel Rossetti discovered a copy of it in the British Museum 20 years afterward and guessed it was by Browning who reluctantly acknowledged it. In the Preface to his Works, Edition of 1868, Browning says: "The first piece in the series I acknowledge and retain with extreme repugnance, and indeed purely of necessity," and goes on to explain that he includes it in order to forestall unauthorized reprints of it.

The poem is dominated entirely by the spirit of Shelley, who is frequently addressed as "Sun-treader," *e.g.*

> "Sun-treader, life and light be thine for ever!"[2]
> "Sun-treader, I believe in God and truth
> And love."[3]

Shelley had come into Browning's life with tremendous force near the end of Browning's sixteenth year,[4] through a copy of a little pirated edition of *Queen Mab* displayed on a second-hand bookstall with a label attached: "Mr. Shelley's Atheistical Poem; very scarce." This the boy bought and devoured. Under its influence,[5] he professed himself an atheist. His mother bought Shelley's works, *i.e.* all of his books of which a copy could be obtained, and presented them to her son on his sixteenth birthday. He soon gave up his atheism, but didn't lose faith in Shelley, thinking he had simply misunderstood him, — which was the case: Shelley is no atheist.

---

[1] At its publication the book received a long notice in the *Monthly Repository* and a notice also in *The Athenæum*.

[2] P. 3, l. 63.   [3] P. 13, ll. 81, 82.

[4] Griffin and Minchin, *Life*, p. 51.

[5] Shelley's long note in connection with his *Queen Mab* also converted Browning to vegetarianism, to which he stuck stubbornly for two years, — until weakened eyesight caused him to abandon it.

Through acquaintance with Shelley's writings, he came also to read Keats.

Pauline, deep-dyed with Shelley's spirit, has both auto-biographical and literary value. And the potency is there of that splendid imagination and intensity of soul which mark the mature work of Browning. Surely, no boy who writes at twenty these lines [1] will fail to write well in later years: To Shelley —

> "Thou must be ever with me, most in gloom
> If such must come, but chiefly when I die,
> For I seem, dying, as one going in the dark
> To fight a giant: but live thou for ever
> And be to all what thou hast been to me!"

9. Browning's first long journey was taken when he was almost 22. Then he went to St. Petersburg on invitation of the Russian Consul-General who had to make a trip to his capital on a special mission. Browning went nominally as his Secretary. The packets of the General Steam Navigation Co. were running from London to Ostend and Rotterdam. Presumably these travellers landed at Rotterdam, but beyond that they were obliged to drive 1500 miles in mail coaches or by private conveyances, to reach their destination. The journey to Russia contributed vastly to the eager mind of Browning, but did not strike the chord in him which Italy did. A visit to north Italy in 1838 brought him under the spell of that country, and he went again for a second visit six years later. He called Italy his university.

10. Returning late in 1844 from his second Italian travel, Browning took up a copy of the *Poems* of Elizabeth Barrett published that summer, and found himself, in *Lady Geraldine's Courtship* (Stanza XLI), classed with Wordsworth and Tennyson. He was much pleased, not only at what was said of himself, but pleased with the

[1] P. 13, ll. 85–89.

Poems in general. The book was meeting with great success, and many were writing to Miss Barrett to express their approval. Urged by John Kenyon, her cousin, Browning finally wrote to her. This began the correspondence which led to their meeting and falling in love. They had been interested in each other's writings for some years and in each other's treatment at the hands of the critics and the public, and each had known something of the attitude of the other. As early as 1841, Mr. Kenyon had desired to introduce Browning to his cousin, but she did not feel physically equal to meeting him.

Elizabeth Barrett had a rare mind but frail health, and had been, when Browning met her, an invalid for seven years, following upon the rupturing of a bloodvessel in the lungs. The Barrett family lived in Wimpole St., London, in a house which her father bought in 1838. After that, she had been in Torquay some time for her health, but it was even further shattered by grief at the drowning of her favorite brother, Edward, who was with her there, in July, 1840. She had gotten back to London and for five years she hardly got out of the house, except for a few hours at rare intervals. Most of the time she did not leave her room, and seldom saw anyone but members of the family. As was inevitable, she was morbid and discouraged, and at the age of 39 (she was six years older than Browning) she considered that her life was over.

Into her illness and gloom came the abounding vitality and love of Robert Browning. She felt keenly that she was unworthy [1] to be a mate for her princely lover. How much she felt the wonder and the beauty of the fact that he loved her may be gathered from her *Sonnets from the Portuguese*. Of course, these have nothing to do with

---

[1] She speaks in this vein in many of the *Sonnets from the Portuguese*.

Portuguese.[1] The name serves as a blind to conceal how they came out of her own life. No more exquisite sonnets are to be found in the English language. They stand undimmed beside Shakespeare's own. They were drawn from her "heart's ground," as she says, in those days when Browning was making love to her. She fought against it for a long time from a sense of duty. Her father was a strange man and very much opposed to any of his children's marrying.[2] When they did so, he practically disowned them. On account of her ill-health, his attitude in her case would be even more severe than in the case of the others. But Robert Browning had found his affinity, and was not the man to be discouraged.

The love-letters of Robert Browning and Elizabeth Barrett have been published [3] by their son. It was a pitiful thing to do. Such letters should be destroyed. They are not for the cold critical public eye. Those letters meant much to the lovers, but they do not mean so much to us. There is in them too little restraint. In Browning's love-poems, no matter how intense the passion, there is splendid restraint. In these letters, one misses the fine element of restraint too much. It is too bad that

---

[1] Browning never saw these Sonnets until the winter after they were married. She slipped the manuscript into his pocket one morning in Pisa. The Sonnets were privately printed at Reading in 1847 without title except "Sonnets by E. B. B." In 1850, they were published with the present title, suggested by Mr. Browning, apropos of his wife's poem *Catarina to Camoens*. What makes the name appropriate is the fact that one of the best sonnet-writers was the great Portuguese poet Camoens (c. 1524–1579). In a library of high rank, I have found these sonnets of Mrs. Browning's catalogued as Translations!

[2] Elizabeth Barrett was the eldest of eleven children. Her mother died in 1828.

[3] *Letters of Robert Browning and Elizabeth Barrett, 1845–1846*, 2 vols. New York, Harper and Bros., 1899.

they were published. But Browning had carefully preserved them, while he had destroyed a great number of
other letters, and his son was not willing that they should
fall into other hands and be published very likely in some
garbled form. He could hardly bring himself to destroy
them. So he gave them to the public in their entirety
exactly as they were. It should be added that they con-
tain much that is of biographical value, besides their
reference to the years 1845–46.

11. In the summer of 1845, Miss Barrett grew stronger,
and her physician thought her able to travel to Italy and
recommended that she should spend the following winter
in Pisa, then a favorite climatic resort. Her father would
not give his consent and continued rigid in his refusal.
Such was the situation for a year. Meantime Robert
Browning continued calling once or twice a week, writing
many letters, and sending her flowers.[1] It was learned
from her father that her going to Italy under any circumstances would be "under his heaviest displeasure," and
it was plain that it would be worse than useless for Browning to ask her father for her hand in marriage. It seemed
to Browning and to her that the circumstances justified
their taking affairs into their own hands. Therefore,
they were secretly married at St. Marylebone Church on
Sept. 12, 1846, and, just a week later, they left for Paris,
where they joined Mrs. Jameson and her niece. After a
week in Paris, they started for Italy, Mrs. Jameson and
her niece with them. They went by way of Orleans and
Lyons to Marseilles, and from there by sea to Leghorn,
and so to Pisa.

---

[1] Cf. the sonnet beginning:

"Beloved, thou hast sent me many flowers,"

No. XLIV, in *Sonnets from the Portuguese* as they now stand.

12. Mr. and Mrs. Browning stayed that winter in Pisa, and in the following April went to Florence. That summer, they occupied for the first time the rooms in the Casa Guidi which in May of the year 1848 became their headquarters, and with which their married life from that time on is associated. They were away much of the time: One summer they visited the towns in the vicinity of the upper east coast of Italy, three summers they were at the Baths of Lucca, four summers they were in England, one summer in France, two summers near Siena, two winters in Paris, four winters in Rome. But they always kept the apartments in the Casa Guidi. It was here that their boy was born Mch. 9, 1849.

13. Mrs. Browning's writings were very successful and brought in some income. But Robert Browning's works had no such experience. All his works before his marriage, except *Strafford*, had been published at the expense of his relatives: His aunt, as we have noted, furnished the money for the publication of *Pauline;* his father paid for the publication of *Paracelsus*, *Sordello*, and all the eight numbers of the *Bells and Pomegranates*. All these books had met with only a small sale at best. He had to borrow £100 from his father at the time of his marriage and journey with his wife to Italy. The chief work of his married life, the two volumes of *Men and Women*, fared somewhat better, but even these volumes did not meet anything like the recognition they deserved. Fortunately Mr. and Mrs. Browning were not dependent on an income from their writings. Mrs. Browning had inherited quite an amount by the will of her uncle Samuel Barrett, and, at the time of her marriage, had £8000 so invested that it yielded £300 a year. Ever after the birth of their son, her cousin John Kenyon had allowed them £100 a year

(against Browning's wishes), and when Mr. Kenyon died in 1856, he left them £11000. So they were able to follow their ideals, without the bread and butter question staring them constantly in the face.

14. Mrs. Browning's health, for years after the marriage, was much improved. Of course, it is very hazardous to marry a sick woman, an invalid. But in this case, the event justified the marriage. Browning's love for her gave her a new lease of life, lifted her out of her melancholy and morbid state, and thrilled her whole nature. Within the next few years she was better than she had ever hoped to be. Her son was strong and well, and became a successful painter. He died at Asolo, July 8, 1912. The fact that it turned out well in Browning's case does not argue in favor of marrying a sick woman. But the fact remains that in this one instance, anyway, the marriage was an immeasurable blessing both to her and to him.

But as years went on, her health declined again, with an occasional severe attack which left her weaker. Gradually travel and social life to which she had grown accustomed became harder for her. Rome was chosen for winter quarters on account of its milder climate. Then came her acute and dangerous illness in Rome in the spring of 1861, the slow and anxious journey to Florence, and her last illness in the Casa Guidi. But even in the last days she was not confined to her room except on June 28. And even on the evening of that day, when Miss Isa Blagden left her, Mrs. Browning said she was better. Her sleep that night was broken and troubled. About daybreak, she awoke and told her husband that she thought she felt stronger. Not knowing that it was the end, she expressed her love for him in words that always afterward lived in his memory. He supported her in his arms, and she grew drowsy and her head fell forward, and she was dead. It was June 29, 1861.

The 15 years of their married life had been exceedingly beautiful, — a unity of soul which is seldom found so nearly complete in this world. There will probably be, in the final reckoning, very few periods of 15 years in any human lives so nearly a perfect union as the married life of Robert Browning and Elizabeth Barrett.

15. With her death Browning was overwhelmed. He could only with the greatest difficulty adjust his mind to life without her. He left Florence that summer and never returned. When he came to London, he could not at first think of keeping house, but finally took the house in Warwick Crescent where he lived for the next 25 years. He made arrangements for the education of his son. He would not surrender to despair, but his desolation was extreme, his life "as grey as the winter sky of London." He shrank from society; it was a year before he could accept invitations as he had done before. By and by, he took what he calls in a letter "a great read at Euripides." He lived in London, but went nearly every summer to France. His father died in 1866, and from that time on Browning and his sister lived together and travelled together. Most of the autumns from 1878 on were spent in Venice. Four autumns Browning and his sister lodged at a quiet inn, the Albergo dell' Universo. But after that they were always guests of Mrs. Arthur Bronson.

16. Beginning early after Mrs. Browning's death and developing with increasing force, was his realization that the power of her spirit was upon him still and that she might "hearken from the realms of help." [1] And so he

---

[1] Browning, *The Ring and the Book*, Invocation, p. 666, l. 77:

"Hail then, and hearken from the realms of help!"

began to weave for her that crown of his maturest and best work, — *The Ring and the Book*, his great Greek pieces (*Balaustion's Adventure* and *Aristophanes' Apology*, with his translation of a tragedy of Euripides contained in each, and then his translation of *The Agamemnon of Æschylus*) — and, beside these, a wealth of short poems, from *Prospice*,[1] written the autumn after her death, to the words,[2]

> "I shall pray: 'Fugitive as precious —
>   Minutes which passed, — return, remain !
> Let earth's old life once more enmesh us,
>   You with old pleasure, me — old pain,
> So we but meet nor part again !'"

in the volume published on the day he died. Mrs. Browning's face looks out through most of the work he did throughout those 28 years from 1861 to his death. At least, if her face does not look out, you know that it is there, — that there is some benediction anciently her smile.[3]

17. All Browning's early writings were poorly received, but this never shook his devotion to his ideals. It took him more than 30 years to win any considerable amount of appreciation,[4] but he kept on just the same. But as the last third of his life drew on, there began to be an awakening to the fact that a man of colossal intellect and power had been at work all these years. Then came Browning's election as Honorary Fellow of Balliol College and his degrees from Oxford, Cambridge, and Edinburgh, and his nomination for the office of Lord Rector of St. Andrews and then of Glasgow University. We cannot

---

[1] Pp. 516, 517.   [2] P. 1295, ll. 51–55, *Speculative*, in *Asolando*.
[3] *The Ring and the Book*, Invocation, p. 667, l. 4 :

> "Some benediction anciently thy smile."

[4] Of course, here and there one liked Browning's writings and recognized his greatness; but such were few for more than 30 years.

cease to be glad that he lived long enough to see some fruit of his toil, to see of the travail of his soul and be, in some measure, satisfied.

18. Mrs. Bronson had a house, built partly on the very wall of Asolo, to which she went to escape the hot weather in Venice. To Asolo, then, on her urgent invitation, came Robert Browning and his sister late in the summer of 1889, on their way to Venice. Here he completed his last volume, which he named *Asolando*.[1] Some of the poems were written here.[2] Then, going to Venice the first of November, Browning had time to read the proofs of the book, and to enjoy his son's home and the city to which he had so often come. There seems to be a singular sense of completeness about it all, as he drew near the end. His last illness was brief, hardly more than two weeks. After an intense and active life of something more than 77 years, he died at ten o'clock on Thursday evening, Dec. 12, 1889, — the very day on which his last volume was published in London. The last day of December that year saw his body laid in the earth under the floor of Westminster Abbey.

[1] The title of the volume Browning explains in the graceful dedication to Mrs. Arthur Bronson, dated Asolo, October 15, 1889. He recalls that Pietro Bembo (made a cardinal in 1539), who had been much in Asolo in the earlier part of his life, is said to have invented a verb, playing upon the name of the town or seeking to find a derivation for it: *Asolare* — "to disport in the open air, amuse one's self at random." On the basis of such a verb, the name of the town, *Asolo*, (1st pers., sing., indic.) would mean "I disport, I amuse myself," and the title *Asolando* would be the gerund, in the dative, "for disporting, for amusing one's self," or more likely the ablative, "by disporting," *i.e.* "by way of disporting" or "by way of amusing one's self at random." The sub-title *Fancies and Facts* indicates the same vein.

[2] See the first sentence in his dedication to Mrs. Bronson. A tablet, placed on the house by the city of Asolo, commemorates Browning's work on *Asolando* there: "In questa casa abito Roberto Browning summo poeta inglese, vi scrisse Asolando, 1889."

Better than any other critic Stopford Brooke has summed up [1] the life of Browning. Only some sentences can be quoted here :

"No fear, no vanity, no complaint of the world, no anger at criticism, no villain fancies disturbed his soul. No laziness, no feebleness in effort injured his work; no desire for money, no faltering of aspiration, no pandering of his gift and genius to please the world, no surrender of art for the sake of fame or filthy lucre, no falseness to his ideal, no base pessimism, no slavery to science, yet no boastful ignorance of its good, no morbid naturalism, no despair of man, no abandonment of the great ideas or disbelief in their mastery, no enfeeblement of reason, no lack of joy and healthy vigor and keen inquiry and passionate interest in humanity. . . . Creative and therefore joyful, receptive and therefore thoughtful, at one with humanity and therefore loving; aspiring to God and believing in God, and therefore steeped to the lips in radiant hope; at one with the past, passionate with the present, and possessing by faith an endless and glorious future — this was a life lived on the top of the wave and moving with its motion from youth to manhood, from manhood to old age. . . . There is no need to mourn for his departure. Nothing feeble has been done, nothing which lowers the note of his life, nothing we can regret as less than his native strength. . . . The sea and sky and mountain glory of the city he loved so well encompassed him with her beauty; and their soft graciousness, their temperate power of joy and life made his departure peaceful. His death added a new fairness to his life. Mankind is fortunate to have so noble a memory, so full and excellent a work, to rest upon and love."

IV. Browning's Published Works

In order to study Browning intelligently, we shall need to bear in mind his chief works as they were published :

1. 1833, *Pauline*, his first published work, — of which

[1] Stopford A. Brooke, in his book *The Poetry of Robert Browning*, last two pages.

we have already spoken sufficiently in our discussion of Browning's life.

2. 1835, *Paracelsus*, a thorough and wonderful philosophical discussion for a boy of 23, on the question : What is the chief end of life — Knowledge or Love?

3. 1837, *Strafford*, a tragedy written at the request of the great actor William C. Macready, and first played by him at Covent Garden Theatre, May 1, 1837.

4. 1840, *Sordello*, a tangled psychological study of the development of a poet's soul.

5. 1841–46, *Bells and Pomegranates*, eight pamphlets. The reason why they came into existence in this shape is interesting : Several pieces of Browning's work — *Pippa Passes, King Victor and King Charles, The Return of the Druses* — lay in his desk. No publisher would take them. Finally he succeeded in arranging with Edward Moxon to bring them out in pamphlet form, very poor type, very cheap paper, each issue to have only 16 pages, two columns to the page. This series Browning whimsically called *Bells and Pomegranates* (catching the words from Ex. 28 : 33, 34 ; cf. 39 : 24–26). And in this pitiful shape appeared the best work of the first half of Browning's life. The eight issues of *Bells and Pomegranates* contained as follows :

No. 1, 1841, *Pippa Passes*.

No. 2, 1842, *King Victor and King Charles*.

No. 3, 1842, *Dramatic Lyrics*.

No. 4, 1843, *The Return of the Druses*.

No. 5, 1843, *A Blot in the 'Scutcheon*.

No. 6, 1844, *Colombe's Birthday*.

No. 7, 1845, *Dramatic Romances and Lyrics*.

No. 8, 1846, *Luria* and *A Soul's Tragedy*.

6. An edition of Browning's collected works, so far, was published in 1849, in two volumes.

7. 1850, *Christmas-Eve and Easter-Day*, two religious poems.

8. 1855, *Men and Women*, 2 vols., 51 short poems in all, some of Browning's best.

9. Browning's *Poetical Works* were published in three vols. in 1863.

10. 1864, *Dramatis Personæ*, short poems.

11. Browning's collected *Works* were published in six vols. in 1868.

12. 1868–69, *The Ring and the Book*, 4 vols., one month apart, Nov. and Dec. 1868, Jan. and Feb. 1869.

13. 1871, *Balaustion's Adventure*, which has in it a translation of the *Alkestis* of Euripides.

14. 1871, *Prince Hohenstiel-Schwangau*, a monologue in the month of the Emperor Napoleon III, discussing his ambitions and his political and social philosophy.

15. 1872, *Fifine at the Fair*, a much more serious and far-reaching analysis of some phases of human nature than some Browning critics have realized.

16. 1873, *Red Cotton Night-Cap Country*, a psychological study founded on facts, *i.e.* on true incidents of a case of dissipation and immorality ("The Mellerio story"). The real names were used at first, but, on legal advice, were changed to fictitious names before publication.

17. 1875, *Aristophanes' Apology*, containing a translation of the *Herakles* of Euripides.

18. 1875, *The Inn Album*, a study of the mind of a woman who still loved the man who wrecked her life.

19. 1876, *Pacchiarotto, and How he Worked in Distemper*, with other short poems. *Pacchiarotto* is an outburst of Browning against his critics.

20. 1877, a translation of *The Agamemnon of Æschylus*.

21. 1878, *La Saisiaz*, a discussion of Immortality, apropos of the sudden death of their friend Miss Anne Egerton Smith who was spending the autumn with Browning and his sister at a villa named La Saisiaz, four or five miles southwest of Geneva, — she died of heart disease on the morning of Sept. 14, 1877.

In the same volume, *The Two Poets of Croisic*, an amusing account, based on historical facts, of how even the most astute literary critics have been fooled.

22. 1879, *Dramatic Idyls*, First Series, short poems.

23. 1880, *Dramatic Idyls*, Second Series.

24. 1883, *Jocoseria*, short poems more or less semi-serious and jesting.

25. 1884, *Ferishtah's Fancies*, bits of philosophy, with lyrics strung between them, some being of great beauty and intensity.

26. 1887, *Parleyings with Certain People of Importance in their Day*. They are dead, but Browning calls them up and talks with them.

27. 1889, (dated 1890 on title page, but published Dec., 1889), *Asolando*, short poems, some of them in Browning's very best vein. This volume was published on the day he died, Dec. 12, 1889.

28. *The Poetical Works of Robert Browning*, in 16 vols., appeared in 1888–89. Browning began making a revision of his poems in the spring of 1888. The edition came out in monthly volumes, completed July, 1889. The poems in his *Asolando* were later included in the 16th vol. of this set, making the whole complete. This is also spoken of as a 17-volume edition, because of having later, in addition to Browning's Works, a 17th volume containing historical notes. In 1894, the 17 volumes were issued also bound in 9 volumes.

It is a vast amount Browning has published, naturally falling into two groups of works: (1) those written before Mrs. Browning's death, and (2) those written after her death, — each with well marked characteristics. Emerson insists that a man's real biography is internal, the story of the development and unfolding of his own mind, and that all outward deeds are secondary. This is certainly true. And you will find the real biography of Robert Browning in his poems. He speaks there by many voices, but you realize after all that he has written down his own soul. These writings, extending over a space of almost 60 years, are one of the richest legacies the nineteenth century has left to the centuries that come after.

V. Some of the Chief Characteristics of Browning's Personality

Browning was a little below medium height, strongly and compactly built, and walked with rapid step. He had bright gray eyes and a ruddy complexion. He talked easily and with vim and clearness.

I look forward to a time when Browning will come into his own, when he will be the favorite poet with men of the world, — business men, engineers, statesmen — men of large affairs. He, of all the poets of the English language, is most of the stripe of the man who is plunged in the world's work. Not one of his portraits looks like the usual notion of a poet. From these portraits, you might judge him to be a prosperous banker, a vigorous member of the House of Commons, a minister of his government to another country, the president of a university, a leading physician, or even the most enthusiastic member of a golf-club. But poet? No. Where is the dreamy eye, the shrinking from the turmoil of the world, the face which tells that the possessor is devoid of common sense? This face belongs to a keen, logical, genial, practical man of the world.

1. The first and most striking characteristic [1] of Robert Browning is *his full-blooded enjoyment of the crush and struggle of humanity*. He could enjoy, as keenly as Wordsworth, the solitudes of the woods and the sea. But he came back always with renewed zest for, and new interest in, the tangled struggle and tumult of cities, factories, business, politics, and the crowd. It was not to him a meaningless scramble, but he saw in it the working of great principles of good and evil, elemental laws which were to be discovered by their results. He saw in all the strife, in all the intrigue, in all the victory and defeat, in all the sin and shame, — he saw the furnace in which human character is made. Facing the furnace, or rather standing in the furnace himself, he declares: [2]

> "This world's no blot for us
> Nor blank; it means intensely and means good:
> To find its meaning is my meat and drink."

The struggle and tumult of the world, its suffering and its sin, instead of repelling him, attracted him, and he rejoiced in it "as a strong man to run a race," or as in the old iron days a soldier exulted in the hour of battle, though it was "with confused noise and garments rolled in blood."

2. This resulted naturally from and was linked with Browning's second great characteristic, — *his universal sympathy*. Everything human was full of interest for him. The more broken and pitiful, the more it attracted

---

[1] The characteristics here given are, of course, drawn from Browning's actions and writings — chiefly from his writings — not from his face, as one who heard this lecture supposed, because his portraits had been mentioned. No wonder that this listener said: "I can't see all that in his face."

[2] P. 450, ll. 41–43, *Fra Lippo Lippi*.

him. Himself a man of stainless character, he never drew
back with "I am holier than thou." I know no one who
mingles justice and mercy so well in his attitude toward
all sorts of sin and shame, except Jesus of Nazareth from
whom Browning learned the way to do it. He shrinks
never from the high and mighty. They also are but men.
To Browning, human personalities are what they are,
without regard to outward seeming, and must stand only
on their own intrinsic worth. He lived for absolute values,
not compromise nor expediency. And he estimates other
personalities by these same absolute values. His sympathy
is more discerning and more universal than Shakespeare's;
for Shakespeare despised the crowd of the common people,
and never touches them except in ridicule. Browning
loved the common people, the struggling masses, as well
as he loved the great and cultured. A single example
will suffice: a factory-girl from the silk mills of Asolo by
her unconscious influence transforms the life and shapes
the destiny of the rich and mighty, as she passes singing
on her one holiday in the year. I refer, of course, to Pippa.

3. A third prominent characteristic is *Browning's im-
patience with mediocrity and his contempt for indecision,
irresolution, half-hearted endeavor, and fear*. No one can
read Browning's poems without feeling his intense virility.
He is so full of red blood himself that the pale-blooded,
white-livered, and passionless folks he cannot endure.
With him, the programme of life is: *decide*, then *act*. He
is fond of rich colors and extreme situations. Porphyria's
lover who strangles her with her long string of yellow hair
that he may keep her just as she is, because he loves her
so, would appeal to few poets as he does to the intense
mind of Robert Browning. If Wordsworth is the poet
of the commonplace things of life, Browning is the poet

of human nature wrought up to its uttermost. Browning, a man of unfaltering courage himself, wanted courage in others. He wants Caponsacchi to thank God for temptation.[1] How else grow strong, except by resistance and overcoming?

> "Why comes temptation but for man to meet
> And master and make crouch beneath his foot?"[1]

Pray not only "Lead us not into temptation" — Browning does not stop there:

> "Yea, but, O Thou whose servants are the bold,
> Lead such temptations by the head and hair,
> Reluctant dragons, up to who dares fight,
> That so he may do battle and have praise!"[1]

Just like Robert Browning to look for men so strong in ideals and inner strength that temptations would be afraid of them.

Everywhere what he wants is no dallying, but decision, action. This has led some purblind critics to imagine that Browning approved of sin, just as some critics have supposed that Jesus approved of dishonesty because he "commended the unjust steward" in the parable:[2] it was only the steward's long-headedness and shrewdness which Jesus commended, not the acts by which he showed it. So Browning distinguishes the quality of soul shown in certain acts from the moral quality of those acts themselves. The most familiar stumbling-stone is *The Statue and the Bust,* in which a man and woman plan an elope-

---

[1] The Pope, in *The Ring and the Book*, p. 854, ll. 51–60. Robert Louis Stevenson ("*Virginibus Puerisque*" *and Other Papers*, London, 1881, p. 43; Medallion Edition, New York, 1909, p. 37) calls this "the noblest passage in one of the noblest books of this century," — *i.e.* now, of course, the century that lately closed.

[2] Luke 16: 1–8.

ment, an adulterous affair, and cherish the plan for years, but never have the courage to carry it out. And Browning condemns them for their failure. It is not that he approves their sinful scheme, but he feels that it was a thing to test their mettle just as much as a better thing would. He has stated this so plainly at the end that I marvel that anyone could miss it:[1]

> "I hear you reproach, ' But delay was best
> For their end was a crime.' — Oh, a crime will do
> As well, I reply, to serve for a test,
> As a virtue golden through and through."

> "Let a man contend to the uttermost
> For his life's set prize, be it what it will!"

This uncompromising view of human life runs through all Browning's works. When we once grasp it, we see the reason often for his choice of subject and manner of treatment. The kind of men Browning admires are men of splendid intensity and the courage to follow their convictions, — Luria, who kills himself in stainless honor rather than submit even to being treated with suspicion; Ivan Ivanovitch, who takes instantly into his own hands the execution of the woman who has saved her own life by the unnatural act of letting the wolves have her children; Herakles, who meets all hardship and all sorrow with a victorious smile and holds "his life out on his hand, for any man to take,"[2]

> "As up he stepped, pursuing duty still
> 'Higher and harder,' as he laughed and said."[2]

Browning feels, as keenly as any man can, "the old woe o' the world" and the pitifulness of the fact that "nothing endures," that "nothing can be as it has been before."

[1] P. 375, ll. 1-4, 17, 18.
[2] *Balaustion's Adventure*, p. 554, ll. 47, 48; p. 556, ll. 74-76.

But he has no idea that this should paralyze our efforts. The unstable quality of life, its constant changefulness, over which so many poets mourn, provokes exultation from Robert Browning:[1]

> "Rejoice that man is hurled
> From change to change unceasingly,
> His soul's wings never furled!"

To Robert Browning, the great men of the world are those who have sternly obeyed God's stern command (so stern that it "clangs"), no matter what the consequences and no matter how soon these men were to be cut off, — that was not their affair — the main point is that they were in the process of the doing, when they were cut off. As "the famous ones of old" throng his imagination, he hears them say:[2]

> "Each of us heard clang God's 'Come!' and each was coming."

4. A fourth very striking characteristic is Browning's *keenness of analysis.* In his examination of human actions, in his search for motives, he is a real psychologist who makes the technical psychology of the schools look poor and artificial. His psychology is pulsing with life and reckons all the tangled lines of hereditary tendency, fresh incentive, fear, hope, passion, which issue in a single act. Among all its scientific men, the nineteenth century did not produce a keener psychologist than Robert Browning. But because his psychological studies were published in the form of live poetry, instead of dry scientific discussions, the scientists did not discover what he had done until many years after he had done it. It is a simple fact that

[1] See *James Lee's Wife*, VI, especially stanzas XI–XVI (pp. 489, 490). The three lines quoted are from p. 490, ll. 8-10.

[2] *Epilogue* to *Ferishtah's Fancies*, p. 1240, l. 38.

he preceded by 20 years the psychological analysis which the scientists finally arrived at, and then they discovered that he had done it better 20 years before. One of the chief reasons why he was so long in meeting with any appreciation is that he was 20 years ahead of the scientific movement of the century. We can have very little patience with this writing of the history of philosophy which reckons only those works that are written in prose and labelled "philosophical dissertations" and ignores the acuter philosophical studies of Goethe, Shakespeare, and many others, simply because they are written more vividly and in metrical form. When the history of psychology shall some time be really written, it will have to take into consideration, not only the technical psychology of the universities, but the work of such men as Robert Browning.

5. And his *comprehensiveness* is the fifth characteristic. Involved in minute analysis as he was, he never lost sight of things in the large, which the scientific analyst almost always does. Browning kept clearly in mind the relation of these minute details to a great whole — he realized that no smallest thing can be isolated, but rather is indissolubly linked with universal laws. And so the sweep of Browning's philosophy is as deep as human life and as wide as the universe to which our human life is everywhere related. There is hardly a phase of life but what Browning has sooner or later reckoned with it and its relations. There is hardly a problem of existence but what Browning has struggled with it, either in his own experience or in imagination. For he had that unusual power of putting himself in another's place and meeting the situation in his imagination almost as keenly as if it were his own life. As a great thinker and as a great philosopher, Browning will hold a first rank, when he comes to be estimated as he is. The

fact is not strange, but a perfectly natural thing, that, when there was no course in Browning given in the English Department of Oberlin College, President King (then a professor — it was before he was made President) gave some study of Browning in the Department of Philosophy.

6. A sixth characteristic is Browning's *faith*. He wanted it to be said of him that at least he "believed in Soul, was very sure of God." [1] The nineteenth century produced many great Christians, but Robert Browning was one of the greatest Christians of them all. At any rate, that is what his own writings show, whatever statements may be made to the contrary.[2] Digging about the roots and questioning the fundamentals of the Christian Religion, he believed more and more in its essence. A man of universal charity toward all forms of religion, his own religious faith as we find it in his poems is singularly simple and beautiful. The proposition made some time ago by the Rev. Dr. John W. Bradshaw,[3] that a course in Browning should be given in theological seminaries, is natural and ought to be carried out. Show me a theological writer who will give young men a vital grip on real religion and a vital message for humanity, equal to that of Robert Browning.

7. And this leads naturally to a seventh characteristic — Browning's *optimism*. We hear much about this, but few realize how deep and far-reaching Browning's optimism is. It is not the optimism of a child, who is optimistic because he knows nothing of life, nor the optimism of that great class who are optimistic because they are comfortable

[1] Near the end of *La Saisiaz*, p. 1132, l. 23.

[2] Cf. discussion of Browning's religious belief in the last chapter of Griffin and Minchin's *Life of Browning*, pp. 294–298.

[3] Dr. Bradshaw was then Pastor of the First Congregational Church of Oberlin. He died in Peoria, Ill., Sept. 2, 1912.

and prosperous and have a good digestion. Browning's is the optimism of a man who knows the worst there is in the world, has probed it to the bottom, and feels to the uttermost the cruelty and the tragedy of life, but who, in spite of all this, believes that God will not be defeated, but that good will triumph at the last. It is the optimism of a man whose eyes are open, who sees the disease and sin and putrefaction of humanity, but is not blind to the forces that make for righteousness, not blind to the reality of some altruism and self-sacrifice already achieved in the history of the world, some nobility of character, some victory of the soul. And these facts, linked with his faith in the Infinite Father, give him the foundations for his hope. Such a man's optimism may well reassure you and me, when we are bewildered and overwhelmed by the evil of the world.

Andrew Lang prefixed to the Butcher-Lang translation (1879) of Homer's Odyssey a sonnet, in which he says that, just

> "As one who for a weary space has lain
> Lulled by the song of Circe and her wine"

would, when he escaped, be

> "glad to know the brine
> Salt on his lips, and the large air again, —"

"So," he says,

> "gladly from the songs of modern speech
> Men turn, and see the stars and feel the free
> Shrill wind,"

and

> "Hear like ocean on a western beach
> The surge and thunder of the Odyssey."

It has seemed to me so strikingly like the way we turn to Robert Browning. Out of the clamor of many voices crying "Lo ! here" and "Lo ! there," out of the pettiness and sentimentalism of those who are writing in our day for a living, out of the cramping and dwarfing clutch of business, out of the arrogant claims of science, out of the specializing in our universities which is fast depriving men of any liberal education, — out of all that is partial and narrow and feeble, we turn to the greatness and serenity and universality and victoriousness of Robert Browning's soul, —

"One who never turned his back but marched breast forward,
  Never doubted clouds would break,
 Never dreamed, though right were worsted, wrong would tri-
    umph,
 Held we fall to rise, are baffled to fight better,
      Sleep to wake." [1]

This brings us to the last main head of our present discussion :

VI. THE INFLUENCES WHICH MADE ROBERT BROWNING WHAT HE WAS

These influences are not far to seek :

1. *His heredity.* On this we have already dwelt in speaking of his father and mother. He had from his parents a good constitution, and from his father especially an exuberant vitality. I have grown more and more to realize, as I look at the world, that sheer vitality is the most needful thing, the greatest source of efficiency, — indispensable to highest success. In a higher stage of civilization, the first essential of education will be the cultivation of physical vitality, and that is a work of more than one generation. Browning's splendid health is what made it possible for him to do the immense amount of

[1] *Epilogue* to *Asolando*, p. 1317, ll. 83–87.

intellectual work which he did, and it was this same health which made life so real to him. The fact is that some people actually *live more* than others do in the same length of time — I know of no other way to describe it, — they have more life in their bodies, life more intense and of a higher potential. Browning had that *plus* condition of energy which, as Emerson teaches, is essential to power. He was, however, of a high-strung nervous temperament, which led him occasionally into outbursts of anger. And his intensity of feeling would have burned him out in early life, if it had not been for the constitution and vitality behind it. From his father, Browning had also great intellectual ability and the artistic instinct. From his mother, again, tenderness, musical taste, reverence, a tendency to mysticism, and yet with this a strain of the German philosophic mind. Such currents combining in Robert Browning gave him a richly endowed personality, unusually versatile and comprehensive.

2. *His education.* His was a real education: *educere*, to lead out; *educate*, to lead out, to develop, the mind of the man. The process of his education stands out in sharp contrast to the dreary artificial mechanism commonly employed and which is too often a system of stuffing, instead of drawing out and developing. Many very thoughtful men have serious misgivings about college education in our day, — each teacher bestirring himself to stuff the students' heads, and the students being mindful chiefly of the possibility of delivering some of the same material again in examination. A college education ought to be of great value to a man, and will be, if he gets from it high purposes, an enlarged area of consciousness, and a discipline of mind which will enable him to master any department of life upon which he may concentrate his

attention. But probably a majority of the students graduate from our colleges without knowing either how to study or how to think. If a man knows how to study and how to think, he can educate himself. The best the college can do for a man is to start him on his self-education. And the serious question is whether the colleges are really accomplishing this. Certain it is that many of the world's greatest minds were self-educated without the college experience. You will see in Stratford-on-Avon the grammar-school where William Shakespeare went to school; it is still used. But he never got any further. His real education was given him by himself, — a few old history books in English translation, a lot of current novels, the streets of London, the audience at the Globe Theatre, and the inner recesses of his own soul, — and the wisest men for 300 years have been trying to stretch their minds to the largeness of Shakespeare's grasp of man's life and the universe. Sir William Herschel, the great astronomer, had a musical education, but instructed himself in mathematics and astronomy, and taught himself to build a telescope and discovered a new planet. Professor Thomas Henry Huxley, one of the most celebrated biologists of the nineteenth century, had a start in the lower schools and then in the hospitals, but chiefly taught the science of biology to himself and then taught it in the universities. Herbert Spencer never had a college education nor had anything to do with the colleges; yet it has been claimed for him that he came nearer to covering the whole field of human knowledge than any man in his day. So with others by the score. Similarly in Robert Browning you have a man largely self-educated by books and travel, a man whose education makes the product of our universities look ignorant. He had, at most, less than two terms in London

University. Yet he reads Greek and Latin at sight for
fun, speaks French and Italian and I know not how many
other languages besides English, and reads Hebrew. He
is, by all odds, the most widely educated man who has
written English poetry. See his Greek pieces, *Balaustion's
Adventure* and *Aristophanes' Apology*, a perfect maze of
intimate knowledge of the classics. See his information
as to history, science, philosophy, art, music, — all mar-
vellously accurate. To read Robert Browning intelligently
is a sort of university education in itself. One can hardly
be surprised that hard-headed men of affairs have very
little respect for the fact that a young man has completed
a college education, with its separation from the real
world, its artificial methods, and its refusal, in the
majority of departments, to see things in the large.
Higher education has to begin with the developing
of certain qualities of mind. And Socrates talking with
the young men in the streets of Athens was, in a sense,
engaged in higher education. And Robert Browning on
his horse, or with the fencing foils, or at his music,
or studying with his tutors, or deep in the books of
his father's library or the British Museum, or travelling
on the Continent, was, all together, laying the foundations of a better education than any university in the
world could give him.

3. *The power of Elizabeth Barrett, his wife.* The influence of personalities is the largest influence in our lives.
I need not speak in detail of other personal influences in
Browning's life — *e.g.* Shelley's which belongs to the
domain of books, Macready's which belongs to the domain
of opportunity — but turn at once to the supreme personal
influence, that of Mrs. Browning. In his relation to her,
he had both of the things which add most to human life,

viz. love and suffering. (*a*) It is useless to argue as to why love enriches and deepens the lives of men and women so much. The fact is that it does. No man need hope ever to be a great artist, a great musician, a great poet, unless he loves greatly. Somehow, that is what stirs the foundations of life, and opens the vistas of the mysteries of the universe. It is literally true that he lives most who loves most. Somewhere in the mystery of human existence, it is probably a fact that love and life are one, and make humanity kindred of the Infinite. (*b*) And if to love be added the bitterness of bereavement, you have the most that can be done for a human personality. It is useless to ask why it is that suffering so deepens our lives and so develops the soul. The fact is that it does. As long as we are comfortable and content, there is no hope of our knowing much about life. But when we are trodden down by the victorious feet of pain and death, then we begin to care for something besides material things, and think of things unseen and eternal. Some portion of such suffering must come to everyone, — to some more than to others. And life is never the same again. There remains nothing but to endure, to think it through, and to reconstruct once more our conception of human life and the universe.

The richest influence in Robert Browning's life was Elizabeth Barrett. His deep reverence for all womanhood became centred upon her. His splendid capacity for loving became utterly devoted to his passionate love for her. Fifteen years of such married life gave him the closest intellectual fellowship. And the loss of her heightened and emphasized the power of her life over him, beyond what would have been possible if she had lived. No doubt he idealized her. She was only a frail woman in a world of mystery, like all humanity, but to him she was the soul of his soul.[1]

She lies buried in the quiet cemetery at Florence. He lies under the feet of the tourists and sightseers who throng Westminster Abbey, — a constant stream of the light, the flippant, and the vain. So much vitality, such keenness for life, such zest in living as Robert Browning had — such love and devotion as Elizabeth Barrett bore toward him — has it all come to dust and ashes? Somehow, it is not easy to think of them as dead. If they are dead, then all the world is an "insubstantial pageant" and may as well dissolve; for there will be none more fit for immortality than Robert Browning and Elizabeth Barrett. But what if they are not dead? What if their passionate intensity of living has its fulfillment otherwhere? What if, as Robert Browning himself confidently expected, they have found

> "the finite love
> Blent and embalmed with the eternal life." [2]

[1] *Prospice*, p. 517, l. 25:

"O thou soul of my soul! I shall clasp thee again."

[2] The Pope, in *The Ring and the Book*, p. 862, ll. 17, 18.

II

INTRODUCTION (CONTINUED): BROWNING AS A LITERARY ARTIST

We turn now to an examination of the Literary Art of Browning.

I. DIFFICULTIES IN THE WAY OF UNDERSTANDING BROWNING

We hear a great deal about the difficulties in understanding Browning. I am sure the obscurity of Browning's writing has been greatly exaggerated, but we may as well discuss at the beginning the real difficulties which the reader of Browning at first meets. These difficulties arise out of five things:

1. The first difficulty which a reader of Browning meets is *the vast amount Browning has written and its very unequal quality*. As we saw, in running over the dates of his published volumes, he has been very industrious from the age of 20 to the age of 77 and has produced an immense amount.[1] The reader hardly knows where to begin and has no idea when he will get through. (*a*) This matter which Browning has published has immense variety. (*b*) Its quality covers wide range, — from the very highest point of poetic imagination to some of the dullest and

[1] It is interesting to notice the distribution of the matter produced — the large amount published in the 12 or 13 years preceding Browning's marriage, the small amount during his married life, and the great amount after Mrs. Browning's death. Cf. the dates of the volumes to see this.

prosiest matter ever strung out in metrical form.   (*c*) Therefore, the fate of the reader is often decided by where he
begins on Browning. If I may give an illustration: A
business man in Cincinnati had heard me say that Browning was the poet for men of affairs, and he made up his
mind to try Browning. But next time I saw him he said:
"I thought you said Browning was good reading. I
couldn't make much out of it." I asked: "What did
you read?" He answered: "That *Red Cotton Night-Cap
Country.*" "Well," I said, "if I told you there was fine
scenery in the state of Colorado, and you began in some
swamp in a corner of the state and saw only that, could
you say you had given Colorado scenery a fair chance?"
No doubt, this gentleman's experience illustrates that of
many. (*d*) Like so many poets (Wordsworth is a striking
example), Browning would have fared better, if he had
written less. If he had written less, or at least had published less, and that had been his best, he would have
met with more success. Browning is more responsible
than anyone else for the feeling against him. He has done
much to defeat himself, because he could not form a just
critical estimate of what he had written, and so failed
to suppress a large number of poems, good as exercises in
philosophy and composition but not such as the public
has patience to wrestle with. (*e*) But this has inevitably
come about from Browning's indifference as to whether
the public approved of him or not. We ought not to say
indifference, because he did care and once in a while breaks
out in indignation against his treatment at the hands of
the critics. But he was a poet for poetry's sake, and the
attitude of his readers toward him was a secondary matter.
The public gave him a cold shoulder from the start. He
went on calmly and persistently, and knowing that the

public were giving no better reception to his best productions than to his worst, he had no standard of public approval or disapproval to judge by, and so published everything which had been born in his own thoughts and had gotten itself written down in poetic form. Meantime, he bore the public no ill feeling and greets them with the jovial words,

> "Such, British Public, ye who like me not,
>   (God love you !) —" [1]

and in another place,

> "So, British Public, who may like me yet,
>   (Marry and amen !)" [2]

But it is a fact that Browning published too much and of too unequal worth. This is a real difficulty for the beginner.

2. A second difficulty is *the colloquial nature of his writing*. Browning is at once more informal and colloquial in style than any of the English poets of first rank. The result is that often what we would understand without hesitation if spoken by a friend we find difficult to understand when we see it on the printed page. (*a*) With the spoken words, the meaning is made evident by emphasis and inflection. But in type, there is no help except in punctuation. Consequently the punctuation of Browning's poems is a matter of extreme difficulty. There is a good story of one occasion when Browning was calling on Thomas Carlyle. And Carlyle was shaving, or something of the sort, and kept his caller waiting a long time. When at last he came in straightening his collar and tie, he said in his gruff way : "Well, Browning, you've taught the English people one

---

[1] *The Ring and the Book*, p. 666, ll. 54, 55. Notice the rest of the sentence.
[2] *The Ring and the Book*, p. 906, ll. 44, 45. The rest of the sentence is good too.

thing anyway — you've taught them the value of punctuation." (*b*) The colloquial nature of Browning's writing results often in the omission of conjunctions. In conversation we say: "Our hope is we shall find a boat," — but how to punctuate that little sentence when it is set up? So we take refuge in printing it in the stilted form: "Our hope is that we shall find a boat." (*c*) More noticeable is the fact that the colloquial style results in the omission of the relative pronoun. We say, "The man I met on the street was John Smith," and it goes all right. But when we write it, it looks queer and we make it read: "The man whom I met on the street." Browning didn't care how it looked; he wrote it down as he would speak it. Consequently, relative pronouns are omitted ruthlessly. I venture to estimate that a large per cent of the difficulty which one has at first with Browning's sentences grows out of the omission of the relative pronoun. There is one solvent which will make plain two-thirds of such cases: Inasmuch as the style is extremely colloquial, read the passage out loud, in a natural conversational way, and you will be surprised to find that what was thick as mud on the printed page is plain and easy when conveyed by the living voice. There is no poet whose writings insist upon being read out loud to be understood, to such an extent as Browning's do.

3. A third source of difficulty in Browning is *the frequent long sentences, of loose structure*, with a large number of subordinate clauses, sometimes with a considerable amount of parenthetical matter, sometimes even with changes of construction, — and always with a picturesque accumulation of all sorts of punctuation marks. Browning can write marvellous short sentences, and has written a host of them. But he has written also a host of long ones

which bear a striking resemblance to the old-fashioned German sentence which is now losing its hold on German authors and lecturers. In dealing with a long sentence of Browning's there is no rule, except to keep a level head, bear in mind what is the chief point he is talking about, and mark the subordinate relation of other parts of the sentence. One presently becomes accustomed to Browning's long sentences and finds little difficulty in them.

4. The fourth source of difficulty is more serious: It is Browning's *vast learning*.

a. Browning is surely the most learned man who ever wrote English verse. That position has been sometimes accorded to John Milton, but you will find Browning's erudition greater than Milton's. Browning's knowledge of the classics is as wide and as minute as Milton's, and he has a vast knowledge of art and mediæval lore which Milton lacks. Browning's knowledge is various and curious, and reaches into a large number of subjects which Milton never touched. I have no fears that Browning's right to the position as the most learned English poet can be challenged.

b. But the trouble is: Browning overestimates his reader's learning. He proceeds upon the assumption that his reader is as familiar with all this varied information as he himself is. Probably Browning never thought anything about it, but simply goes ahead, disregards the reader, and puts down what is plain to Browning and would be, he supposes, plain to anyone. But alas! we are not Browning; our education has been in the narrow channel of American schools and colleges, and Robert Browning has the better of us. Consequently, what is a matter of course to him has to be dug out by us, with searching.

c. This everyday familiarity which Browning has with a wide range of learning is the reason why his allusions are sometimes so obscure. A few illustrations out of hundreds:

(1) He is very fond of the Latin poet Horace, — quotes him and alludes to him often, but is more likely to call him *Flaccus* [1] than Horace. Who of us, unless one just out of the Latin class, remembers that that poet's name is Quintus Horatius Flaccus, or knows who Flaccus is?

(2) An obscure artist, whose "name and fame" Browning himself says "none of you know," is spoken of as "the imaginative Sienese great in the scenic backgrounds." [2] Fortunately in his second reference [3] to this "etcher of those prints," he gives the man's name, Ademollo.

(3) The *Summa Theologiæ* of St. Thomas Aquinas is mentioned familiarly as the "Summa." [4] That work is the standard of theology in the Roman Catholic Church, but who, except the Latin clergy and those outside of that communion who make a special study of theology, would know what book is meant?

(4) Browning puts into the mouth of Count Guido's brother the line:

"There's a *sors*, there's a right Virgilian dip!" [5]

How many who read Virgil in high school or college ever know that it was once a custom to dip into Virgil at random for guidance, just as some very pious people nowadays open their Bible believing that they will be directed to the verse that will make plain to them what to do?

[1] *e.g.* p. 803, l. 13; p. 824, l. 56; p. 826, l. 11.
[2] P. 650, ll. 42–48, especially ll. 46–48.
[3] P. 654, ll. 37–40.
[4] *e.g.* p. 743, l. 65; p. 758, ll. 50, 66.
[5] P. 731, l. 70.

(5) Again, we read:

> "All
> Glories that met upon the tragic stage
> When the Third Poet's tread surprised the Two." [1]

To whom does this refer? "The Two" are Æschylus and Sophocles. "The Third Poet" is Euripides.

(6) A point is made [2] of the Jewish scribe's treatment of the ineffable name [3] of the God of the Hebrews, when he came to it in his reading in the synagogue. Who, except Old Testament students, knows that the scribe was not allowed to pronounce the name, but substituted for it another word — *Adonai*, Lord?

And so on in hundreds of cases with no effort to make the allusion clear. The illustrations we have chosen are simpler than many others and take less time to explain. Browning often writes with a perfect tangle of allusions to mythology, history, literature, and science. We do not mean to imply that the majority of such allusions are obscure, but unfortunately, to most of us, many of them are.

d. Browning's knowledge of the history of painting makes him sometimes write so that hardly any but those who have been educated specially in that line can get the full benefit of the poem, *e.g. Old Pictures in Florence.* One must have something of Browning's own artistic instinct to appreciate fully such interpretations of artists' struggles and ideals as he has given in *Pictor Ignotus,*

---

[1] P. 860, ll. 65–67.

[2] P. 755, l. 83–p. 756, l. 9.

[3] The consonants of the name are known — JHVH, or YHWH, according to what scheme of transliteration you adopt, — pronounced probably Yahweh, certainly *not* Jehovah, which is a word no ancient Hebrew ever heard of; that word was invented about the time of the Protestant Reformation in the 16th century A.D.

Fra Lippo Lippi, and *Andrea del Sarto*, or to realize how fine a thing is a little poem like that one called *A Face*.

e. Browning is so thoroughly at home in music that one needs a course in that subject to comprehend fully his frequent references to it [1] and similes drawn from it, or to get the full force of such poems as *A Toccata of Galuppi's*, *Master Hughes of Saxe-Gotha*, *Abt Vogler*, or his parleying *With Charles Avison*, the great organist.

f. Browning's knowledge of so many languages creates a difficulty for us who have so few languages at command. It is not that Browning likes to parade them, but he very naturally flings in phrases from other languages familiar to him, especially if they give atmosphere and local color. So the reader of Browning must be prepared for Greek — we need Greek even in reading his translations from Greek into English, they keep the Greek idiom so much — Latin in abundance, plenty of French of course, some German (not many German words used), and in all poems laid in Italy a great number of Italian expressions. Browning is fond of Hebrew and Aramaic, and in two poems, *The Melon-Seller* and *Two Camels*, he has had the audacity to put the Hebrew expressions in the Hebrew characters.[2] Usually a writer, if he quotes Hebrew words for the general reader, transliterates into the Roman alphabet; so few, except those who study the Old Testament in the original, or read rabbinic writings, or are familiar with Yiddish, can be supposed to read the Hebrew characters.

---

[1] *e.g.* in *Fifine at the Fair*, p. 944, ll. 19–24.

[2] P. 1219, ll. 2, 3; p. 1229, l. 28, — see also the Hebrew word in l. 34. Cf. Browning's note in connection with another poem, p. 1214, where he quotes the title of a rabbinic treatise and also a proverb, both in Hebrew letters. Browning writes only the consonants, which is the more general usage. The vowel-points when written are placed under the consonants. Hebrew reads from right to left.

g. It is Browning's wide and varied learning and his great number of interests that makes his style diffuse. Browning lacks critical judgment. He does not know how to reject. His mind is so well stored that, when he starts to write, his head is full of similes, metaphors, analogies, associations, suggested trains of thought. All of these are more or less related to the subject in hand, and a good critical judgment would dictate which should be kept and which rejected. But as they crowd upon Browning, he puts them all down on paper. The result is often distracting and confusing. He would have gained much if he had left out much. The poems are often too long, twice as long as need be — twice as long as they would be, if he had left out the more irrelevant parts. Browning himself does not lose the connection of thought, but the reader often does. Often one might drop out a page, two pages, three pages, — and the next line joins right on and goes on just as if nothing had happened. It was only one of those little excursions of Browning's into a field which was suggested at that point by something he was saying. Browning is constantly under the temptation to wander off into philosophizing — excellent philosophizing it often is, but aside from his story. He enjoys searching out motives and seeing how small acts are related to the universe. He has great intellectual keenness in doing this. But the story has to wait, and the general style of the whole is often made too discursive. It is true that, as one grows familiar with Browning's poems, this easy meandering style grows to have a certain pleasure in it, but it is often confusing for the reader at first.

5. A fifth source of difficulty is *the monologue form* in which so many of the poems are cast. It is true that Browning has narratives told in the third person, also that

he has a large amount written in dialogue form. But all
his best poems are in monologue, *i.e.* he speaks through
the mouth of the man or woman whose deeds or thoughts
are being told and the narrative is, therefore, in the first
person. I remember that this seemed queer to me at first,
— so many voices telling, in their own person, their adventures and their thoughts. Yet, as soon as you get
accustomed to it, this form of presentation does not even
attract your attention. The narrative in the first person
is far more vivid than any in the third person can be.
Browning is not a successful dramatist, but he is the most
successful writer of monologues. What Shakespeare has
done for the drama Browning has done for the monologue,
— has brought it to the highest point it has reached in
English Literature.

The difficulties in reading Browning, though usually
exaggerated, are real: The vast amount and unequal
quality of Browning's work, the colloquial nature of his
style, the frequent long and involved sentences, his own
great learning and overestimate of the reader's learning, and
the monologue form in which many of the poems are cast.

II. Excellences in Browning as a Literary Artist

I have grown more and more doubtful about all the
statements usually made about Browning's literary ability.
Nothing is more full of superstitions than the world of
literary criticism. Some man succeeds in getting before
the public a number of statements in regard to an author
and these become accepted, and then are repeated *ad
infinitum* by those who come after, because it is easier
to do that than to read the author and see for one's self.
Thus there become settled literary superstitions, — that
such and such an author has such and such failings and

only such and such points in his favor. It is the old trick
of the average critic — he has not read the book. Sometimes when a man looks for himself, he is surprised. The
usual estimate of Browning's skill is simply one of the
ruts of criticism. Has it occurred to you that it may be
partly due to the fact that the critics who first established
it may not have been widely enough acquainted with
Literature and so condemned as inartistic what was simply
unfamiliar to them?[1] Not long ago, in studying for
another course without regard to Browning, it fell to me
to go through a good number of books on English metre.
And I found, in books written from different standpoints
and following different methods of inquiry, that, when
it came to discussing rare and difficult metres, often metres
imported from other languages, they frequently had to
cite Robert Browning for examples.[2] It is quite probable
that Browning's literary reputation has suffered because
many of his metres are unfamiliar. But we must say
that it is not fair to suppose a man unskilled and lawless,
when he is working often in metres too difficult for most
poets to use. Anyway, I have come more and more to
doubt the sweeping statements made in many books and
periodicals, about the literary skill shown in Browning's
poems. There are a few points of excellence in Browning
from the standpoint of his craftsmanship in English poetry,
and these I would like to mention now.

[1] Cf. the musical critics' treatment of Richard Wagner when his operas
first appeared.

[2] *e.g.* F. B. Gummere, *A Handbook of Poetics*, Boston, 1898, pp. 203, 207,
209; T. S. Omond, *A Study of Metre*, London, 1903, p. 64; J. B. Mayor,
A Handbook of Modern English Metre, Cambridge, 1903, pp. 27, 81, 142,
145. For a thorough discussion of Browning's metres, see Geo. Saintsbury,
A History of English Prosody, London, 1906-10, vol. III, pp. 216-240;
cf. pp. 296-301, especially pp. 299, 300.

1. *His choice of words.* I don't know anyone in English Literature who chooses words that give so much in one word as Robert Browning does, — a whole picture in one word. It seems unnecessary to point out single examples. It is his habit when writing at his best. But I will cite a few instances out of hundreds. The *Italics* in the illustrations are our own, to call attention to the words under discussion.

a. In the poem entitled *By the Fire-side*, the man who speaks the lines imagines what he will do when he gets to be old — he will sit there by the fire "deep in Greek" — but his mind will run away from the Greek up into the Apennines, back to that day with the sweetheart of his youth. Then he gives us details of the picture in which every stanza is a work of art. But we pause at the first two lines of stanza VIII : [1]

> "A turn, and we stand in the heart of things;
> The woods are round us, *heaped* and dim."

Anyone who has been in the Alps or Apennines knows how accurately these words tell the tale. In a tramp of six weeks in the higher valleys of Switzerland, not less than a hundred times where valleys narrowed down these words came and no others would cover it — mountains on every side — "we stand in the heart of things" — "woods heaped and dim." Nothing but that word *heaped* could describe the woods on the steep slopes and spurs and knolls — *heaped*, that's how they look.

b. The poem "*Childe Roland to the Dark Tower Came*" was written in one day and not afterward revised. It has some stanzas that are not poetry at all and some that are of the most consummate poetry to be found. The

[1] P. 246, ll. 1, 2.

knight, Sir Roland, walks across the dreariest plain which imagination can devise and is surprised by coming upon "a sudden little river." Notice this part of the description of the stream : [1]

> "All along,
> Low scrubby alders *kneeled down* over it."

Have you ever heard any expression which could convey that picture like the words "*kneeled down* over it"? You have seen it — you know how a brook cuts across a level pasture or meadow, and the steep banks are three or four feet high, and how the alders grow out from the bank near the water-line and then bend sharply to grow upright. How often we have noticed that bend in the stock of the bush, six or eight inches from where it comes out of the ground, almost exactly like the crook of a knee, — so that, glancing at it from the side, not bothering our minds as to how it came to be so, we see the alder *kneel down* over the water.

c. In the same poem, stanza XXX, when at last suddenly the knight realizes that he has reached the place he has been years searching for : [2]

> "*Burningly* it came on me all at once,
> This was the place !"

"*Burningly* it came" — Any of us who have noticed what comes with a sudden realization of something that concerns us deeply — the flush of heat which goes over the whole body, often making one break out in a perspiration even in a cold day — will know that all that is told, sharply and conclusively, in

> "*Burningly* it came on me all at once."

---

[1] P. 377, ll. 34, 35, in stanza xx.   [2] P. 378, ll. 25, 26.

d. Or take the line from *In a Balcony:* [1]

"As yonder mists *curdling* before the moon."

Could any other word create in the mind the picture created by that word *curdling?* We have all seen the thing, but I doubt if any man in literature has described it so accurately as Browning has in the words

"yonder mists *curdling* before the moon."

e. This facility in using the most expressive word or phrase to convey the picture vividly is one of the commonest things in Browning's writing, and the expression is so apt that, once you get it in mind, the thing itself always calls up Browning's words.

(1) How many times every autumn a day comes that brings to my mind the lines from poem VII of *James Lee's Wife:* [2]

"Oh, good gigantic smile o' the brown old earth,
        This autumn morning!"

(2) How often on days when the breeze pours over the hills and plains have the words come, from Browning's *Two in the Campagna:* [3]

"An everlasting wash of air."

(3) By the seaside, over and over again come the lines from *Balaustion's Adventure:* [4]

"Beside
The sea, which somehow tempts the life in us
To come trip over its white waste of waves,
And try escape from earth, and fleet as free."

---

[1] P. 481, l. 78.   [2] P. 490, ll. 21, 22.   [3] P. 251, l. 9.
[4] P. 574, ll. 1-4. In line 4, "and fleet as free," *i.e.* as free as the foam itself.

Most of us feel the drawing of the sea, but I do not know where to find anything that gets at the very essence of it as Browning does when he writes that the sea "*somehow tempts the life in us.*"

(4) Or take a summer day with keen breeze and unusually clear air, and dark blue sky with only now and then some deep fragment of white cloud voyaging across it, and the words of the same Greek girl in *Aristophanes' Apology* will haunt your memory: [1]

> "Greed and strife,
> Hatred and cark and care, what place have they
> In yon blue liberality of heaven?"

You will go far before you find words that tell what you're looking at on such a day, as do the words "*yon blue liberality of heaven.*"

But an unusual skill in the choice of words is really a habit with Robert Browning. So we need not dwell on it any more.

2. *His wealth of diction.* Of this only a few observations:

a. Browning's vocabulary is astonishingly large and varied. I don't believe it is exceeded by any except Shakespeare's. Unfortunately, as already noticed, it contains much besides a strictly English vocabulary. It is a sort of cosmopolitan vocabulary. But fortunately, what is strictly English in it is of very wide range.

b. Browning does not hesitate to coin words when he needs them, or thinks he needs them, *e.g.*

(1) "malleolable" [2] — From Latin *malleus*, a hammer, we have *malleable*, capable of being shaped by the blows of a hammer. But Browning wants a more discriminating word. So from *malleolus*, the diminutive of *malleus*, he

---

[1] P. 576, ll. 1–3.
[2] In *The Ring and the Book*, p. 658, l. 44.

gets *malleolable*, capable of being shaped by blows of a
little hammer.

(2) "unstridulosity"[1] — We have the adjective *stridulous*, making a sharp creaking sound, the verb *stridulate*,
the noun *stridulation*, and so on. But we do not find in
any of the dictionaries either *stridulosity* or *unstridulosity*.
Browning, however, supposes from *stridulous* a noun
stridulosity which would mean the act, or quality, of being
stridulous, *i.e.* the giving of a creaking sound (but a sense
somewhat different from that of *stridulation*), and then he
uses a negative prefix and makes *unstridulosity*, the absence of such an act, or quality. He uses the word figuratively in the connection, meaning simply the quietness
of the man, while the others "creak, creak, creak." (See
ll. following.)

(3) "un-mouse-colours"[2] — This is a compilation, of
course. From the verb to *color* and the noun *mouse-
color*, Browning supposes a verb to *mouse-color* and then
prefixes *un-* and gets a verb to *un-mouse-color*, *i.e.* to take
the mouse-color off from the skin of the oxen referred to
in the passage.

But these coinings are mentioned here chiefly as curiosi-
ties. The main point has to do with words that are standard English.

c. Browning knows how to use words so as to give an
impression of great wealth and beauty of diction, perhaps
surpassed only by Shelley at his best (as *e.g.* in *Adonais*).
By way of illustration:

(1) In *The Last Ride Together*, stanza III, the description
of a sunset:[3]

> "Hush! if you saw some western cloud
> All billowy-bosomed, over-bowed

[1] In *Prince Hohenstiel-Schwangau*, p. 922, l. 78.
[2] In *Prince Hohenstiel-Schwangau*, p. 930, l. 12.   [3] P. 352, ll. 43–46.

> By many benedictions — sun's
> And moon's and evening-star's at once —"

(2) The beginning of *Johannes Agricola in Meditation:* [1]

> "There's heaven above, and night by night
>   I look right through its gorgeous roof;
> No suns and moons though e'er so bright
>   Avail to stop me; splendour-proof
>   I keep the broods of stars aloof:
> For I intend to get to God,
>   For 'tis to God I speed so fast,
> For in God's breast, my own abode,
>   Those shoals of dazzling glory passed,
>   I lay my spirit down at last."

And so in an immense number of instances.

3. And in *the drawing of pictures* on a larger scale than in single words and phrases, Browning excels. This is related, of course, both to his choice of words and to his wealth of diction. His poems abound in vividness, — scenes cut out like cameos and quite unforgettable — some humorous, some serious, but all showing this skill. In that little poem *By the Fire-side* are a dozen word-pictures, any one of them worth transferring to canvas in crayon. In *Love among the Ruins*, you can see just how the country looks,[2]

> "Where the quiet-coloured end of evening smiles
>   Miles and miles."

In *Evelyn Hope*, you can see the darkened room and the streaming in of the

> "two long rays thro' the hinge's chink." [3]

In his longer poems there is a lavish abundance of word-pictures, *e.g.* the autumn evening in *Sordello:* [4]

[1] P. 445, ll. 10–19.   [2] P. 229, ll. 65, 66.
[3] P. 229, l. 16.   [4] P. 104, ll. 37–41.

> "A last remains of sunset dimly burned
> O'er the far forests, like a torch-flame turned
> By the wind back upon its bearer's hand
> In one long flare of crimson; as a brand,
> The woods beneath lay black."

You will find this quality in Browning's writings almost anywhere, but perhaps more strikingly in *Paracelsus* and *The Ring and the Book*.

4. And a fourth excellence is *the beauty and melody of his lines*.

a. It is usually charged that Robert Browning cannot write musical lines. This charge has been passed from mouth to mouth until it is widely believed. But the fact that once everybody believed that the world was flat didn't make it so. And the repetition of the statement that Browning's verses are not musical doesn't make it so. The longer I have read Browning the more I have come to doubt such statements. There's music and music — there's the Jew's harp and there's the pipe-organ.

b. Now, Browning did write a large number of harsh lines of blank verse and usually did it on purpose, because the harsh line conveyed an impression of the condition described; *e.g.* in the beginning of *The Ring and the Book*, a line which can be cited as unusually harsh: he speaks of a ring found

> "After a dropping April; found alive
> Spark-like 'mid unearthed slope-side figtree-roots
> That roof old tombs at Chiusi."

That line [1]

> "Spark-like 'mid unearthed slope-side figtree-roots"

is certainly rough enough. But, bless you, would smooth lines convey the impression of the torn up condition of

[1] P. 649, l. 5.

the ground where the ring is found after the rain? It
seems to me that the harsh torn line goes with the torn
soil. So with a host of illustrations.

It is true that Browning did not polish his blank verse
so much as Tennyson did, but he has the stronger vigor of
lines on that account. And the harshness of his lines has
been grossly exaggerated. If you'll pardon the reference
to myself: I repeated, some time ago, a mass of *The Ring
and the Book* (three-quarters of Caponsacchi's monologue),
an hour and a half of it, in a college town in Michigan.
And students in the Senior Class went to their Professor
of English and said: "How's this? We understood that
Browning's lines are rough and harsh. We couldn't see
it in that hour and a half of them." On the contrary,
you will look long to find anything superior in melody to
great blocks of Browning's blank verse in *The Ring and
the Book*, not simply in Caponsacchi's speech but also in
Pompilia's monologue or the Pope's. There is not time
to quote, but I may start a few:

(1) P. 783, ll. 43 sqq.,

> "There was a fancy came."

(2) P. 796, ll. 44 sqq.,

> "And, all day, I sent prayer like incense up."

(3) Almost anywhere on pp. 798–802, the closing part of
Pompilia's monologue. Begin *e.g.* with p. 798, l. 5,

> "For me
> 'Tis otherwise; let men take, sift my thoughts,"

or p. 800, l. 55,

> "For that most woeful man my husband once,"

or p. 801, l. 47,

> "O lover of my life, O soldier-saint."

(4) The Pope, p. 852, ll. 37 sqq.,

> "First of the first,
> Such I pronounce Pompilia."

You will notice the melody also in many other monologues of *The Ring and the Book*, and in *Cleon, Andrea del Sarto, A Death in the Desert,* and other blank verse pieces. I might add the lines from *Balaustion's Adventure:* [1]

> "Whereat the softened eyes
> Of the lost maidenhood that lingered still
> Straying among the flowers in Sicily."

But there is no use in multiplying illustrations to substantiate a fact that is perfectly obvious.

c. And in short poems Browning has abundance of melody.

(1) We have only to think of the long vibrating lines of *Abt Vogler,* flexible as a whiplash, *e.g.* [2]

> "Therefore to whom turn I but to Thee, the ineffable Name?
> Builder and maker, Thou, of houses not made with hands!"

or the beauty of the long line and short line combination in *Love among the Ruins,* or the effect of many of his lyrics, such as "I send my heart up to thee, all my heart," [3] or "Dance, yellows and whites and reds." [4]

(2) And Browning has done what they've all been trying to do — make the movement of the lines themselves reflect the thing described or narrated. Thus, *e.g.* in the little poem *Meeting at Night.* [5] The picture in the first stanza is what some of you have seen when coming in at evening on the coast. Now start to read the stanza out loud:

---

[1] P. 573, ll. 32–34.
[2] P. 500, ll. 25, 26.
[3] The first song of *In a Gondola*, p. 346, ll. 21–27.
[4] At end of the parleying with *Gerard de Lairesse*, p. 1276, ll. 67–75.
[5] P. 228, ll. 15–26.

> "The grey sea and the long black land;
> And the yellow half-moon large and low;"

and the long vowels and liquid consonants make these
two lines move slowly in spite of you. But the rapidity
of the third and fourth lines is very evident, the voice
quickening involuntarily with the sharp consonants and
the increased proportion of short vowels:

> "And the startled little waves that leap
> In fiery ringlets from their sleep."

This all corresponds exactly to the scene — sea and land
and moon all serene, and then our attention suddenly
attracted by the dancing waves at the bow of the boat —
these more noticeable in the shallow water just as the
boat strikes the sand. The second stanza accomplishes
much the same thing: Lines 1 and 2 move slowly and
serenely, as the man crosses "a mile of warm sea-scented
beach" and "three fields," — both are lines in which
long vowels prevail, — but lines 3 and 4, describing what
happens at the house, move quickly with an accumulation
of such words as "tap," "quick," "scratch," "spurt,"
"match," — all with short vowels and crisp consonants.
The poem is a masterly piece of work, but the technique
with which it is done nowhere obtrudes. Of course, in
any such work, the finer the technique the more it serves
the thought, but the less attention it attracts to itself, —
and perfect technique would attract no attention at all.
Such is the irony of art.

(3) Browning's short poems, again, are not so polished
as Tennyson's. But often they are very effective by
reason of sheer ruggedness.

d. I am sure that many of Browning's harsh and curious
rhymes are made in fun. They always occur in some

serio-comic thing like *The Heretic's Tragedy* or *A Grammarian's Funeral*, or in some jovial thing like *Old Pictures in Florence* or *A Likeness* or the Prologue to *Ferishtah's Fancies*, or in some sarcastic thing like *Pacchiarotto*. Someone ought to get out a book on Browning's humorous vein.[1] He was so human that he couldn't help seeing the funny side to some things which are really very serious and many things which have serious pretensions. The mixture of humor and seriousness in many of his poems, just as it exists in human life, is very interesting. And it is quite plain that in some poems he purposely exaggerates the funny side; and some poems, of course, are altogether jocular in tone. But many critics have not had the saving grace of humor themselves and so have taken in downright earnest what Browning means as a humorous exercise. So they are inclined to think him a poor artist when what he is drawing is intended to be nothing but a caricature. The ridiculous rhymes in *A Grammarian's Funeral* are simply to help out the grotesqueness of the whole thing. To understand them so is altogether in keeping with the pedantic tone of the man in whose mouth the poem is put. And the grotesqueness is, no doubt, quite true to the extravagances of these first students in the Revival of Learning. So we get "cock-crow . . . rock-row," [2] "overcome it . . . summit," [3] "fabric . . . dab brick," [4] " far gain . . . bargain," [5] "failure . . . pale lure," [6] "loosened . . . dew send." [7] And the rhymes in *A Likeness* are atrocious, *e.g.*[8]

[1] Vida Dutton Scudder has done something of this in her book *The Life of the Spirit in the Modern English Poets*, Boston, 1895, pp. 201–238.

[2] P. 366, ll. 56–58. [3] P. 366, ll. 68–70.

[4] P. 367, ll. 36–38. [5] P. 367, ll. 64–66.

[6] P. 367, ll. 76–78. [7] P. 368, ll. 12–14.

[8] P. 518, ll. 75–78.

> "That hair's not so bad, where the gloss is,
> But they've made the girl's nose a proboscis:
> Jane Lamb, that we danced with at Vichy!
> What, is not she Jane?   Then, who is she?"

So are the performances in the Prologue to *Ferishtah's Fancies*, "Italy" rhyming "spit ally,"[1] "unpalatable" — "each who's able,"[2] "masticate" — "peptics' state."[3] Now, no one with common sense can suppose that these things were done otherwise than on purpose to be in keeping with the spirit of these poems.   Whether that's wit or not is another question, but it is not to be charged up to awkwardness and careless workmanship.

5. Browning's great *use of alliteration* ought to be mentioned.   Examples are hardly needed:

> "Or, August's hair afloat in filmy fire."[4]
> "I see the same stone strength of white despair."[5]
> "Some dervish desert-spectre, swordsman, saint."[6]

Referring again to presenting Caponsacchi before an audience, — on more than one occasion people have spoken to me of noticing the immense prevalence of alliteration as they listened.   If illustrations from Caponsacchi are desired:

> "In glided a masked muffled mystery,
> Laid lightly a letter on the opened book."[7]

> "Out of the coach into the inn I bore
> The motionless and breathless pure and pale
> Pompilia."[8]

> "Still breathless, motionless, sleep's self,
> Wax-white, seraphic, saturate with the sun."[9]

[1] P. 1217, ll. 2–4.
[2] P. 1217, ll. 22–24.
[3] P. 1217, ll. 29–31.
[4] P. 666, l. 30.
[5] P. 882, l. 66.
[6] P. 911, l. 29.
[7] P. 758, ll. 72, 73.
[8] P. 770, ll. 31–33.
[9] P. 771, ll. 66, 67.

In the last two illustrations we have not only initial alliteration, but, in "breathless" and "motionless," we have final
alliteration in -*less*.

There is such a thing as overdoing alliteration, and
Browning may be in danger of that, although his alliteration seldom produces anything except a pleasant effect
— a sense of melody and harmony.[1]

6. One more point must be spoken of among the ex-
cellences of Browning's literary art, and that is *cadence
of lines*. In his blank verse, he manages cadence with
great skill. Cadence (literally, *falling*) is a thing that
can't be taught. It must lie in the soul of the poet. It
is not so much in the words as in the atmosphere of the
line. It is that which makes you realize that things are
coming to a conclusion. In single lines, it is that which
causes the voice to drop in spite of you and creates in your
thoughts a sense that the poet has written something
ultimate. For a case of prolonged cadence, one should
be familiar with the last 50 lines of Pompilia's monologue
in *The Ring and the Book*. For the finest cadence Browning ever wrote in a single line, take this from *Cleon:* [2]

"Within the eventual element of calm."

Few poets have been able to handle cadence, and the
greatest poets have written only a few such lines. The
two most famous lines for cadence are probably Milton's,
in *Sampson Agonistes,* [3]

[1] Prof. John B. Nykerk, in conversation, has raised the question whether
Browning was influenced by Old English alliterative verse, or, leaving the
O. E. literature out of account, whether it may not be possible that certain
elements of personality and tendency to grapple with life, which developed the
alliterative verse-form in Anglo-Saxon days, may be the same that produce
in Browning's poems such a high degree of alliteration.

[2] P. 468, l. 32.

[3] *Sampson Agonistes*, l. 598, (Cambridge Ed., Boston, 1899, p. 301).

> "And I shall shortly be with them that rest,"

and Tennyson's, in *Guinevere*,[1]

> "To where beyond these voices there is peace."

But it seems to me the cadence in this line of Browning's is fully equal to that in the others.

> "And I shall shortly be with them that rest."
> "To where beyond these voices there is peace."
> "Within the eventual element of calm."

Surely Browning's line is as good as the best.

7. *Poetic imagination* is closely related to craftsmanship in the art of verse. The first essential is that a man have somewhat to write, and fundamental to this is poetic imagination. But the subject is too large to be discussed here. It may be added, however, that in extent, daring, and vividness, Browning's imagination is equal to that of the greatest poets of the world. This is plain in the whole conception and handling of his work. Even those who grudge to concede to Browning a firstclass skill in versification are obliged to pay their tribute to his mind. Certainly his works show on every page the vast power of an imagination which is creative and life-giving in the highest degree.

In choice of words, then, in wealth of diction, in ability to draw word-pictures, in beauty and melody of lines, in use of alliteration, and in the producing of cadence, we find Browning a literary artist of high rank. And in poetic imagination, he is without a superior.

---

[1] The last line of *Guinevere* in the *Idylls of the King*, (Globe Ed., New York 1892, p. 458).

III

INTRODUCTION (CONCLUDED): OUR PLAN OF STUDY IN THIS COURSE

A WORD about our plan of study in this course.

1. There is no way to understand Browning except by reading Browning and reading a large amount of Browning. This brings our minds into harmony with his, and we understand him easily. Nothing can ever take the place of this.

2. The surest rule for dealing with a passage which is difficult to understand is the rule already in vogue among Browning students: Read it. If you don't understand it, read it again. If you don't understand it then, read it again. If still you don't understand it, read it again. And read it until you do understand it. This is scientific. The trouble is that either the thought or the method of expressing it is unusual. Therefore, we need to have our minds tuned up to it. By reading it we are tuning our minds up to Browning's when he wrote it, — and presently it is plain and easy to us.

3. These principles, that the only way to understand Browning is to read much of him and to read till we understand, will govern our study in this course.

4. Our general plan will be to go from short poems to the longer and more complex ones. Sometimes I shall

have to assign more than we can discuss in class. We
will begin with some of the short poems next time.[1]

[1] In the college classes, at the close of each lecture, the poems to be discussed at the next meeting of the class have been assigned. The assignment
has grouped the shorter poems and could usually be read in two hours,
though sometimes it would take more. Reading once the assignments
has been required. Students have been also advised to read twice, if possible,
all assignments, *i.e.* before the lecture dealing with them and after the
lecture. Twice reading could not, of course, be required, because of time
consumed in once reading the Browning assignment and in attending to
the outside reading. In examination, each student has had to answer
whether he has done all the reading assigned in Browning's works and outside
of Browning's works.

IV

SOME OF THE SHORT POEMS PUBLISHED BEFORE MRS. BROWNING'S DEATH

THE titles of Browning's volumes as they appeared have been preserved as headings of the divisions in his collected works, with only one modification.[1] But many short poems are not now found under the general heading which corresponds to the volume in which they first appeared. This is on account of the redistribution made by Browning in his collected works of 1863 and 1868. Thus, *e.g. Men and Women*, 2 vols., when published in 1855, contained 51 poems. Now only 13 are left standing in that division of his works, and of these only eight were in the original *Men and Women*, the other five being three that appeared in *Dramatic Lyrics*, 1842, and two from *Dramatic Romances and Lyrics*, 1845. At the same time, 43 poems that appeared in *Men and Women* in 1855 are now distributed under several different divisions of the collected works. This was done, of course, simply because Browning, having his works before him, saw that these poems, by reason of subject and treatment, belong more appropriately under other general heads. *Men and Women* is cited simply as an illustration of the shaking up which took place in all the volumes of short poems.[2] The matter

[1] *Dramatic Romances and Lyrics*, 1845, has been shortened to simply *Dramatic Romances*.

[2] The short poems published in volumes subsequent to 1868 stand now in the works under the titles of those volumes, and in the same order in which they first appeared.

78

is mentioned here to avoid confusion in the mind of the reader, when he notices that, in the following comment on some of the short poems, a poem is said to have been published in a certain volume, and then finds the poem now in an entirely different division of Browning's works.

I. Cavalier Tunes, pp. 219, 220

Published in *Dramatic Lyrics*, 1842.

1. These songs are set in the war between King Charles I, of England, and the Parliament, 1642–45. The cavaliers who sing them are on the King's side.

2. The songs are full of references to the men of the time: King Charles (born 1600, crowned 1625, beheaded 1649) and his opponents — Oliver Cromwell (1599–1658), John Pym (1584–1643), John Hampden (1594–1643), Sir Arthur Hazelrig (died 1661), Nathaniel Fiennes (1608–1669), "Young Harry" (beheaded 1662) son of Sir Henry Vane. Prince Rupert of Bavaria (1619–1682), grandson of James I, went to England at the beginning of the Civil War to help the cause of his uncle, King Charles. His coming appears in the first song, encouraging the cavaliers. "Kentish Sir Byng" is some knight from Kent, no historical person.

3. These are real soldier-songs. Songs in Literature put into the mouths of soldiers are usually too literary, and too soft and musical. These are rough songs such as real soldiers might sing. The historical names mentioned are names that were in everyone's mouth in those days. The songs have plenty of rough soldier-spirit, with sneers at the Puritans on account of their short hair ("crop-headed Parliament" in the first song, "Roundheads" in the third song), with Cromwell's nickname "Noll" (for Oliver), and with the use of such words as

"the devil" and "hell" without which a soldier's song would be feeble, and even a stronger word when Cromwell's troopers are mentioned in the second song. The word "carles" (twice in first song) means churls — the two words are doublets from Old English *ceorl*.

4. Browning has given to the chorus of the third song the movement of galloping horses, *i.e.* it certainly seems as if the line

"Boot, saddle, to horse, and away!"

gallops as you read it.

II. THE LOST LEADER, p. 220

Published 1845, in *Dramatic Romances and Lyrics*.

The poem refers to one who deserts the people's cause. The poem is a severe one. From the fact that it mentions Shakespeare, Milton, Burns, Shelley, as being on the people's side, it is natural to suppose that the recreant is a literary man. Wordsworth fills the bill, — a liberal in his youth and intensely moved by the French Revolution — in later years opposing innovations and progressive legislation. In 1875, Browning was asked if he referred to Wordsworth in the poem and answered:[1] "I have been asked the question you now address me with, and as duly answered, I can't remember how many times. There is no sort of objection to one more assurance, or rather confession, on my part, that I *did* in my hasty youth presume to use the great and venerable personality of Wordsworth as a sort of painter's model; one from which this or the other particular feature may be selected and turned to account."

[1] We quote only a part of the letter. It was printed in Grosart's Edition of Wordsworth's *Prose Works*, and is reprinted in Berdoe, *Browning Cyclopædia*, pp. 256, 257.

III. GARDEN FANCIES, pp. 222–224

These were first printed in *Hood's Magazine*, July, 1844, and then were included in *Dramatic Romances and Lyrics*, 1845.

1. The first one, *The Flower's Name*, is made up of the thoughts of a lover as he walks again where he walked in the garden with his sweetheart, where so many things are associated with her, but especially the flower whose name she told him. The poem is gentle and delicate.

2. The second, *Sibrandus Schafnaburgensis*, is full of exuberant humor, drawing the contrast between a dead book of philosophy and the real world of living things.

a. The title is the name of the author of the old book supposed to be brought into the garden. Griffin and Minchin, in their *Life of Browning*, point out that he met such names in reading as a boy Nathaniel Wanley's *Wonders of the Little World* [1] in his father's library. *Schafnaburgensis* means a native of the city of Aschaffenburg, on the river Main in the province of Lower Franconia in Bavaria.

b. The poem is so fine a thing that we are justified in adding these notes:

P. 223, l. 44. The punctuation at the end of this line in the Globe Edition should be a comma instead of a period. The sentence runs on into the next stanza.

l. 46, *arbute*, arbutus, a genus of evergreen shrubs, of the heath family. There are several species. This is probably the most common one, called the "strawberry tree" from its fruit which outwardly resembles the strawberry. Not to be confused with the "trailing arbutus" of the U. S. A.

---

[1] Wanley's book was published in 1678. There are also editions of 1774 and 1806–07.

laurustine, (also spelled laurestine), *Viburnum tinus*, an evergreen shrub or tree of the south of Europe; it flowers during the winter months.

l. 50, *Stonehenge*, on Salisbury Plain eight miles north of Salisbury. The remains, supposed to be of Druid origin, consist of upright stones and some horizontal slabs. The original plan of the whole can be made out. A traveller might well be tempted to count the stones.

l. 55, *pont-levis*, drawbridge (literally, light bridge).

l. 66, *Chablis*, a town in France in the department of Yonne, famous for its wines — hence *Chablis*, wine from this place. Not to be confused with Chablais [1] in Savoy.

l. 67, *oaf*, a repulsive elf, used here figuratively for the book.

l. 68, *Rabelais*, François Rabelais (1495–1553), great scholar and humorist of the Renaissance, evidently a favorite with Browning.[2]

l. 70, *limbo*, a supposed border land somewhere between Heaven and Hell, where certain souls have to await judgment. Hence any place apart from the world, place of confinement.

l. 72, *akimbo*, with elbows sticking out and hands on hips.

ll. 74, 75, *de profundis, accentibus lœtis, cantate!*, out of the depths sing with joyful tones, (or accents).

P. 224, l. 2, *right of trover*, right to a thing that is found. Laws of trover refer to possession of things one finds in highways and such places.

l. 11, *John Knox*, 1505–1572, Scottish reformer, severe Presbyterian, very Puritanical, *e.g.* his volume, 1558,

---

[1] Cf. *A Likeness*, p. 518, l. 67, "And the chamois-horns ('shot in the Chablais')."

[2] Cf. *A Likeness*, p. 518, l. 70, "And the little edition of Rabelais."

entitled *Blasts of the Trumpet against the Monstrous Regiment of Women.* Of course, nothing could be more ludicrous than John Knox fastened into the front row in an opera house and obliged to witness a ballet.

l. 17, *sufficit*, it is enough.

c. According to the poem, Browning (or whoever is speaker of the lines) reads the old dry book conscientiously

> "From title-page to closing line,"

and then proceeds to his revenge. This consists in dumping the book down the hollow trunk of an old plum-tree. That was "last month." Some days have passed, and meantime the book has lain there among the rain-drippings and all the wild creatures that inhabit the decaying inside of the old tree. The buoyant fancy of Browning revels in the contrast between the dead book and the living things. This morning, he fishes up the book with a rake and promises it a return to his shelf where it can

> "Dry-rot at ease till the Judgment-day."

d. The poem abounds in gentle irony. This dreary book is called "our friend," "my bookshelf's magnate," "his delectable treatise."

e. The poem should be read many times. It will be found highly rejuvenating to drooping spirits. Only a few lines need be quoted as samples:

(1) The spider whose web had been woven across the hole in the tree:

> "Now, this morning, betwixt the moss
> And gum that locked our friend in limbo,
> A spider had spun his web across,
> And sat in the midst with arms akimbo."

(2) Everyone knows how disastrous to the appearance

of a book a wetting is, but no one has ever told it more skilfully than Browning here:

> "Here you have it, dry in the sun,
> With all the binding all of a blister,
> And great blue spots where the ink has run,
> And reddish streaks that wink and glister
> O'er the page so beautifully yellow:
> Oh, well have the droppings played their tricks!"

Then comes a very funny turn — did this dry-as-dust philosopher of long ago know anything about things that have become associated with his book?

> "Did he guess how toadstools grow, this fellow?
> Here's one stuck in his chapter six!"

(3) Then follows that turning loose of the poet's imagination as to the incongruous experiences of the old book,

> "when the live creatures
> Tickled and toused and browsed him all over,"

in the midst of

> "All that life and fun and romping,
> All that frisking and twisting and coupling."

It partakes of Browning's sympathy with all forms of life.

IV. Meeting at Night, Parting at Morning, p. 228

Published in *Dramatic Romances and Lyrics*, 1845.

1. These are certainly two exquisite bits of scenery, and something besides.

2. Browning has the courage to make them true and vivid, where a poet given to more polishing would have removed them from reality. Thus, if the over-nice object to such phrases as "the slushy sand" and the "blue spurt" of the match, they must remember that the sand at the water's edge is simply *slushy* and that the "blue spurt"

of the phosphorus and sulphur match (the kind of match everybody used to have) is what we saw evening after evening. I am reminded of a discussion between some theological students, objecting to the preacher's having said in an illustration that the tide was out and the boats were "stuck in the mud," — the discussion being chiefly how to say the boats were stuck in the mud without saying they were stuck in the mud. There's too much of that nonsense, and Robert Browning would have none of it. He used the words that convey accurately what he was describing.

3. The remarkable quality of *Meeting at Night* has been referred to in our discussion of Browning's literary art. We might call attention to how true to life is the woman's sitting in the dusk waiting for the man to come and lighting the lamp at his tap on the window-pane. The passionate greeting in the last two lines should not be overlooked, her voice less loud than the beating of their hearts.

4. *Parting at Morning* is not such a piece of art as *Meeting at Night*, but it is a worthwhile bit nevertheless. The tide is coming in rapidly — it seems as if the sea comes round the cape of a sudden. The sun comes up over the mountains to the eastward, making a path of gold across the water toward the observer — it is "a path of gold for him," *i.e.* for the sun, as if he were going to travel across the world on the path of gold that is on the water, (*straight*, probably the adjective, predicate after *was*, but maybe the adverb, *straightway*). With the coming of the tide and the sun, the man must hasten back to his business and struggle in the city.

5. Both poems are in the mouth of the man, *not* the second one in the mouth of the woman as Dr. Berdoe [1]

[1] Berdoe, *Browning Cyclopædia*, ed. 1912, p. 270.

supposes. "Him" means the sun. The point is that even as the sun goes forth for the day along his golden path, so the man must needs go forth into the "world of men." No wonder that, with such a start, Berdoe finds the fourth line "slightly obscure."

V. EVELYN HOPE, p. 229

Published in 1855 in *Men and Women*, vol. I.

1. It is a poem of great intensity. The lover asks us to come and sit by the side of this sixteen-year-old girl where she lies dead, and he succeeds in speaking to us for two stanzas about her, but the rest of the poem is addressed to her. Though he was "thrice as old" as she and though their "paths in the world diverged so wide," he loved her and will love her forever.

2. Stanzas V, VI, and VII would be plainer to us if the punctuation were such as we are accustomed to, *i.e.* with what he intends to say at last to Evelyn Hope enclosed in quotation marks, thus *e.g.*

> When, "Evelyn Hope, what meant," I shall say.

The quotation ends with the fourth line of stanza V, and he goes on to say what he will learn. Then the quotation is resumed with stanza VI, "I have lived," I shall say, and continues to the middle of stanza VII. The remaining four lines are addressed to her now, and would be outside the quotation.

3. We are not to understand from stanzas IV, V, and VI that Browning believes in metempsychosis. He does not give in his support to that doctrine. But the point is that *even if* it is so and he has to be reincarnated over and over again — give himself up and live the life of different men in different ages and different lands — *even if* that is

true, one thing will persist through all his various existences, and that will be his love for Evelyn Hope. And
throughout all his existences he will want her, and when
he finds her at last, he will refer to "the years long still"
"in the lower earth" when his "heart seemed full as it
could hold." But it was not full without her:

> "There was place and to spare for the frank young smile,
>   And the red young mouth, and the hair's young gold."

And he will tell her:

> "I loved you, Evelyn, all the while."

4. The reader is not to suppose that he has autobiography
here. We are in contact with Browning's intense personality, but poets in writing love-poems do not necessarily
draw on their own definite experience. Such is the poet's
imagination.

5. The more this poem is read the more its extraordinary
vividness strikes us. Perhaps no detail contributes more
than does the piece of geranium picked by her own hand,
still standing in the glass of water but beginning to die too.
The geranium is not a poetic and romantic flower, and
most poets would avoid it. But Robert Browning is
writing of life as it is, and knowing how common geraniums are (or used to be) as house-plants, he puts in a piece
of one of Evelyn Hope's geraniums as a true bit of the
setting. For this sort of thing we honor him.

VI. LOVE AMONG THE RUINS, pp. 229, 230

Published in 1855, the first poem in vol. I of *Men and
Women*.

1. It contrasts the glory and power and ostentation
that have been with the love of a girl — the love that

now is, — and finds "love is best." It is a singularly
graceful and attractive poem.

2. A few notes may be of use:

a. Consideration shifts alternately from what *was* when
the scene was a populous city to what *is* now — just a
few ruins [1] and a girl. The emphasis should be strong
upon *then* and *now* and all words which distinguish the
past from the present, *e.g.* "*he* looked," "*she* looks now,"
"*they* sent," — so that the two parts will not be confused
but each will furnish background for the other.

b. Browning, of course, always scorns the pedantic
rules set down in rhetoric books, about prepositions at
the end of clauses and sentences. So in this poem (stanzas
I and II) he has (1) "its prince . . . held his court in,"
where elaborately written prose would go: in which its
prince held his court; (2) "slopes of verdure, certain rills
. . . intersect and give a name to," — slopes of verdure
which certain rills intersect and to which they give a name;
and (3) "a wall . . . made of marble, men might march
on," — a wall on which men might march.

c. The latter half of stanza III — Browning expects
that men in the old days were as now, — with hearts
pricked up by desire for glory, struck tame by dread of
shame, and susceptible to the power of gold — having
their price, as cynics say every man has now.

d. Stanza V — *fleece*, meaning that which is covered
by fleece viz. the flock of sheep; *girl with eager eyes and
yellow hair*, Browning seems fond of yellow-haired girls,
cf. Porphyria.[2]

e. Stanza VI — There should be no mistake about the
third and fourth lines. Many editions do not print cor-

---

[1] In fact, only the basement of the great tower remains (stanza IV).

[2] In *Porphyria's Lover*, p. 375, ll. 43, 45, 64.

rectly *glades'*, possessive plural — the colonnades of the glades. There were temples on the mountains in the distance (none near, stanza II) and there were colonnades in the glades. *Causeys*, causeways. In the latter half of the stanza — notice that there will be two kinds of embraces: (1) *first* her eyes will embrace his face, (2) then the lover and the girl will embrace each other.

f. Stanza VII — As to the pillar built to their gods by the ancient inhabitants: (1) The pillar was made of the brass of captured chariots (chariots captured by these million fighters sent out in a single year), and yet in spite of using so many they were able to reserve a thousand chariots which were specially fine, being ornamented with gold. This makes "Gold, of course" apply to these 1000 chariots. (2) It may be, however, that "Gold, of course" has nothing to do with "chariots," but means simply an additional item as to the wealth of the city: "Of course there was plenty of gold," even though a million men were sent to war in a single year. (3) Further, it may be that the brazen pillar has nothing to do with captured chariots (although such use of such spoils would be quite consistent with ancient customs), and that the 1000 chariots reserved are a thousand of the king's own, *i.e.* although he sent 1,000,000 men to war that year, he could still reserve 1000 chariots at home. The words "in full force" favor this interpretation.

As to the latter part of this stanza: (1) It may be that "Earth's returns etc." is in apposition with "blood that freezes etc." *i.e.* "blood that freezes etc." is all there really is of the wealth and glory. (2) Or it may more likely be that "Oh heart! oh blood that freezes etc." is this lover's own heart and blood, and that the exclamation "Earth's returns etc." is independent and means: such are earth's returns — these ruins here. (3) In either case, "Shut them in" is addressed to nobody in particular, exactly as "let them go" might be, and means practically "let them be," "let them alone," — the "them" being those who struggled in those "centuries of folly, noise and sin." How he esteems what they struggled for is shown by his mentioning a couple of items and then dismissing it with the words "and the rest." In contrast to it all, love in the present hour is best.

3. This belief in the beauty of life in the present hour and this doctrine that love is best are very like so much of Browning. This is a good love-poem. Of course, if people don't want love-poems, they mustn't read them. But if we're going to have love-poems at all, let's have them red-blooded and intense. No pale-blooded love-poem is worth writing or worth reading.

VII. "DE GUSTIBUS —" pp. 238, 239

Published in vol. II of *Men and Women*, 1855.

1. The title is a part of the Latin proverb "De gustibus non disputandum est," there should be no dispute concerning tastes (literally, concerning tastes it must not be disputed).

2. This is a bit of humor. The point is: if the soul after death keeps the same tastes it had while in the body, then the ghost of each will walk in the places he used to like most. Thus the ghost of the lover of trees will walk in an English lane — and then with that alertness which is always in Browning's best work, he sees the ghost of such a tree-lover walking in the lane,

"By a cornfield-side a-flutter with poppies,"

and urges him to get out of the way, so as not to frighten the boy and girl making love in the hazel coppice. Anyone accustomed to walking in English lanes knows how often you come upon the boy and girl making love. We should not miss Browning's sympathy with them nor the sadness of the fact that youth is so soon over:

> "And let them pass, as they will too soon,
>   With the bean-flowers' boon,
>   And the blackbird's tune,
>   And May, and June!"

3. Every ghost to the spot he liked best before he became a ghost. Therefore, Robert Browning's ghost will go to Italy, for

> "What I love best in all the world
>   Is a castle, precipice-encurled,
>   In a gash of the wind-grieved Apennine."

So his ghost will very likely be around a place like that, or else

> "In a sea-side house to the farther South."

We hardly need to call attention to the picturesqueness of the *gash* in the mountain and the precipice *curling* about the castle, and of each of the details of the scene further south, each detail chosen not for elegance but to be exactly true to Browning's memory of such places, and ending with the bare-footed girl and her melons and her anarchistic sympathies, true to what Browning knew so well of many of the Italian peasants.

4. Apropos of this confession, as to whither his tastes turn, Browning breaks out,

> "Italy, my Italy!"

And catching at Queen Mary's [1] words about Calais, he writes:

> "Open my heart and you will see
>   Graved inside of it, 'Italy.'
>   Such lovers old are I and she:
>   So it always was, so shall ever be!"

[1] Mary Tudor, Queen of England from 1553 to 1558.

VIII. Home-Thoughts, from Abroad; Home-Thoughts, from the Sea, p. 239

Published in *Dramatic Romances and Lyrics*, 1845. They were at that time arranged under one heading *Home Thoughts from Abroad*, the first as "Oh, to be in England" and the other as "Nobly Cape St. Vincent," and between them was another, "Here's to Nelson's Memory," which is now placed as the third poem under *Nationality in Drinks* (p. 222).

1. *Home-Thoughts from Abroad* are the thoughts of an Englishman, who is away where the "gaudy melon-flower" is (probably in Italy), as the English spring comes up before his mind's eye. He describes it beautifully. If there is one thing in the poem finer than the rest, it is the reference to the thrush and the exquisite fancy as to why he sings as he does:

> "That's the wise thrush; he sings each song twice over,
>   Lest you should think he never could recapture
>   The first fine careless rapture!"

2. *Home-Thoughts from the Sea* are the thoughts of an Englishman at sight of Trafalgar, where Lord Nelson won the great victory over the combined fleets of France and Spain on Oct. 21, 1805, and Gibraltar, which has been held since 1704 as one of the bulwarks of the British Empire. With fresh realization of what Trafalgar and Gibraltar mean, he says:

> "Here and here did England help me: how can I help England?"

He wants everyone to ask that question — everyone who turns as he turns, this evening, to God, "to praise and pray." Any normal Englishman ought to have his patriotism and his religious thinking stirred by passing Trafalgar and Gibraltar.

"The first four lines of *Home-Thoughts from the Sea* are an exact transcript of the scene which he [Browning] beheld from the deck of the *Norham Castle* on the evening of Friday, 27 April, 1838, on his first voyage to Italy." [1]

IX. BY THE FIRE-SIDE, pp. 245–248

Published in vol. I of *Men and Women*, 1855.

1. The situation is just this: The man looks forward to "life's November" — what will he be doing then? Why, he will be sitting by the fire "deep in Greek." And "the young ones" (probably grandchildren), seeing him so absorbed will slip away to cut "from the hazels" a mainmast for their "ship." He will forget his book, however, and his thoughts will go back to that day in the Apennines with the woman he loved, when their two lives were poured together into one life forevermore. His mind goes over again each detail of the scene and each incident of their walk. The poem is really addressed to the same woman, his wife, who sits opposite him at the fireside. So, at the end, his thoughts come back from that event of the past and gather about her now. He reiterates his intention of having that crowning evening to think about in the autumn of his life.

2. It is hardly too much to say that the poem, from first to last, is altogether delightful and wonderful. It is useless to try to make quotations from it, because there is no good place to stop.

3. The place described is probably a gorge near the Baths of Lucca. The Brownings had spent the summer at the Baths of Lucca in 1849 and again in 1853. The wife sits yonder, (stanza LII),

> "Musing by fire-light, that great brow
> And the spirit-small hand propping it."

[1] Griffin and Minchin, *Life of Browning*, p. 127.

This describes Mrs. Browning. That is a curious fancy — a "spirit-small hand," *i.e.* a hand as small as a spirit has. It is true, of course, that Browning proposed to his wife in London, not in a gorge in the Apennines. But it is also undoubtedly true that we have here a confession of his love for her and how much it has meant to him. It is simply a case of putting the truth of his own love into a natural setting of which he was fond, viz. this mountain gorge.

X. THE GUARDIAN-ANGEL, pp. 257, 258

Published in vol. II of *Men and Women*, 1855.

1. Subtitle, *A Picture at Fano*. (*a*) Fano is a city at the mouth of the river Metauro, in the province of Urbino-and-Pesaro, on the east coast of Italy. (*b*) Robert Browning and his wife visited Fano in the summer of 1848 — stayed three days there and then went to Ancona. (*c*) The painting referred to is by an artist of Bologna, named Giovanni Francesco Barbieri (1590–1666), called Guercino ("squint-eyed"), and by this nickname he is generally known, — "Guercino drew this angel" (stanza VI). (*d*) The picture is on a tomb in the church of St. Augustine. It represents a little child at prayer, while an angel stands over him, with wings outspread, the left arm around the child, the right hand closing over the child's clasped hands. (*e*) Three times Mr. and Mrs. Browning went to this church to sit and look at this picture (stanza VII). (*f*) The poem was evidently written at Ancona (stanza VIII, last line).

2. Protestants have discarded the doctrine that there is a guardian angel for each one of us, but Catholics devoutly hold it. Browning feels keenly how beautiful a thing it would be to have that angel, when done with the child, step out of the picture over to him and do for him what

is being done for the child.   Only Browning needs it more, world-worn as he is.

3. The poem goes to pieces toward the end.   The friend spoken of in stanza VI is Alfred Domett, who went to New Zealand and settled in 1842.   He is the man called *Waring* in the poem of that title (pp. 348–351).   The Wairoa (stanza VIII) is a river in New Zealand.   The last three stanzas are distracted between Mrs. Browning and Alfred Domett, and are a poor ending, diverting attention from the point.

4. But the first five stanzas are addressed directly to the angel on the tomb, and are very discerning.   They come to a good conclusion and should be read as a poem by themselves.   There will come times in any tired man's life when he will deeply appreciate them.

XI. THE PATRIOT, p. 333

Published in vol. I of *Men and Women*, 1855.

1. The subtitle is *An Old Story*.   And it certainly is an old and oft-repeated story how men have done their utmost to help their country and have come to the hangman's rope or the headsman's axe.   The leaders of the American Revolution of 1776 knew what they were facing; it is related that they said grimly: "We must hang together or we'll hang separately."   Of course, George Washington was a traitor to the British crown.   But, being successful in leading the American colonists, he became "the father of his country."   Furthermore, there are plenty of examples of the fickleness of the populace, — on a man's side when he's winning, deserting him when he fails.   This also is an old story.

2. In the case described in the poem, a man has in whole-souled devotion given himself for his country, — at first

successfully, attended by great applause at his entry into the city, but later the tide has turned against him and now he is on his way out to be hanged. Very naturally the contrast is bitter in his thoughts, between how he entered exactly a year ago and how he goes out to-day. And the contrast could not easily be better described than Browning does it. A year ago,

> "It was roses, roses, all the way,
> With myrtle mixed in my path like mad,"

and house-roofs loaded with people, church-spires flaming with flags, the sound of so many bells that they filled the air like a mist, and the old walls rocking with the crowd and their cheering. If he had asked them to give him the sun from the skies, they would have agreed at once to take it down and give it to him, and immediately would have asked him what else he wanted. He realizes now that it was he who leaped at the sun to get it and give it to the people, *i.e.* he tried to do for them a great thing, tried to bring great blessing to their lives, and was not able to reach it. Now, a year to the very day from that temporary triumph, he is walking through the streets to his execution. The crowd are on their way to the scaffold at the Shambles' Gate. A few with palsy cannot go, but sit at the windows to see him pass. It rains, and the rope cuts his wrists tied behind him. Anyone who cares to flings a stone at him. He thinks by the feeling that he is bleeding at a wound in the forehead, where a stone has hit him. Sharply the two scenes come to his mind — a year ago and now:

> "Thus I entered, and thus I go!"

"Well," he thinks, "cases have been known where a man in a triumph, overcome by the excitement, has dropped dead. If I had died that day a year ago and had gone up before God fresh from the approbation of men, I might have been told by God that I had been paid by the world and might have been questioned by God: 'What dost thou owe me?' Now surely I have not been paid by the world. I have done the best I could for my countrymen and what I get is a hanging." The balance is on the other side of the account:

"'Tis God shall repay: I am safer so."

"So," *i.e.* safer trusting God's award than men's.

This paraphrase purposely avoids quoting more completely the phrases in the poem. They are full of extraordinary vividness. This patriot is a fine figure of a man who has held unfalteringly to his ideal and is therefore ready to stand unashamed before God.

XII. The Last Ride Together, pp. 352, 353

Published in vol. I of *Men and Women*, 1855.

1. The circumstances are plain: The lover has been rejected. He accepts it philosophically, and asks the lady to take just one more ride with him, which she agrees to do. He helps her on her horse, (this is the point in stanza III, cf. the last two lines when he is helping her on), and they begin to ride. He doesn't worry about the fact that she has rejected his suit, nor about the fact that he's never going to ride with her again. Enough that he's riding with her now, and he makes the most of it. What's the use in spoiling the present hour by thinking about what has been and what is to be. The main point is that he's riding with her, and that's better for him than soldiers' glory or artists' fame. He has this one chance, and (stanza II)

"Who knows but the world may end to-night?"

And as they ride, it seems to him that Heaven may be only (stanza x)

> "The instant made eternity."

Such a perpetuation of this instant would be quite satisfactory to him.

2. The poem is one of Browning's best expressions of his belief in making the most of the hour that now is. It is also one of the richest of his short poems in melody and beauty.

XIII. A GRAMMARIAN'S FUNERAL, pp. 366–368

Published in vol. II of *Men and Women*, 1855.

1. This is a piece of rare and curious humor.

2. The circumstances are plain:

a. The time is indicated by the words Browning has put under the title: "Shortly after the Revival of Learning in Europe."

b. A Renaissance scholar, whose study has run chiefly to Greek, is now dead, and is borne on the shoulders of his students to burial on a high mountain, the only fit place for burying a man of such high thinking and such high aspirations. The poem is spoken by the leader of the students, as they go on: he begins while they are still on the plain, continues as they come into a city on the mountain-side and march through its market-place, still continues as they wind up the narrow way beyond, and ceases speaking soon after they reach "the platform" [1] on the summit.

c. The poem consists of eulogy of their dead teacher,

---

[1] P. 368, l. 3, "Well, here's the platform." What is this platform? Is it something built up on which the body is to rest permanently, in a sarcophagus? Or is it a temporary structure on which they are to hold a funeral service? Or does it mean simply the level spot on top of the mountain?

wise and pithy sayings about life (chiefly suggested by his attitude toward life), and parenthetical directions and exhortations to the bearers and other students.

3. The poem gives an accurate reflection of the interesting mixture of pedantry, real sense, and grotesque exaggeration among these first students in the Revival of Learning. Throughout the poem the realization is keen of the pitiful disproportion between the work a scholar puts in and the visible results achieved. This must always be so.

4. Notice some words:

a. Academic terms:

P. 367, l. 16, *he gowned him,* became a student, put on a scholar's gown. Such was the custom in the Middle Ages and the Renaissance. Whatever use of distinctive academic dress survives in our day owes its origin in some sort to this old custom.

l. 26, *the comment,* commentary written in the margin of manuscripts. Learning is spoken of here figuratively as a book, and to go thoroughly one must read not only the text but the marginal comment.

b. Medical terms:

P. 367, l. 30, *queasy,* nauseated, — used of his mind's devouring everything nor ever getting too much — never getting sick of it. (Not a strictly medical term as the next one is.)

l. 52, *Calculus,* regular medical term for stone, whether in the liver, kidney, bladder, or any other organ of the body. The word is more commonly met in the plural *calculi.*

l. 54, *Tussis,* a cough.

l. 61, *soul-hydroptic.* The more common word is *hydropic* (direct from Latin *hydropicus,* which in turn comes directly from the Greek), but *hydroptic* is found (made from English *hydropsy*, erroneously following *epilepsy, epileptic*, and the like). *Hydroptic*, dropsical. The point is that in some dropsical conditions there is much thirst, and this man's soul is as thirsty as if it had the dropsy.

c. Greek words :

P. 367, l. 95, *Hoti*, ὅτι, conjunction, *that, because.*

l. 96, *Oun*, οὖν, conjunction, *then, therefore.*

P. 368, l. 1, *the enclitic De*, δε, inseparable unaccented particle, — not to be confused with the word δέ which means *but.*

d. Why does Browning use such words as these we've been speaking of ? Of course, to give atmosphere and color to the poem.

5. According to the poem, the reason why the dead scholar gave himself so unreservedly to his work and denied himself the immediate comfort and good of life was because he wanted the greater good, the "far gain." And he believed that he would not fail of that, because he had confidence that death would not be the end :

> "Others mistrust and say, 'But time escapes :
>   Live now or never !'
> He said, 'What's time? Leave Now for dogs and apes !
>   Man has Forever.'"

XIV. PORPHYRIA'S LOVER, p. 375

First printed in *The Monthly Repository*[1] in 1836,[2] under the title *Porphyria* and over the signature "Z." In the same number of *The Monthly Repository* appeared *Johannes Agricola* (now called *Johannes Agricola in Meditation*). In *Dramatic Lyrics*, 1842, these two poems were

---

[1] Edited by Browning's friend the Rev. W. J. Fox, who had hailed *Pauline* with a long notice in 1833.

[2] New series, vol. X, pp. 43, 44.

yoked together, without individual titles, under one heading *Madhouse Cells; Johannes Agricola* was No I, and *Porphyria* No. II. In the edition of his works in 1863, Browning abandoned the heading *Madhouse Cells. Johannes Agricola in Meditation* now stands among *Men and Women*, p. 445.

1. Porphyria's lover loves her desperately, but is evidently not her social equal (ll. 46–50) and is not sure that his love is requited (ll. 57–60) and is sullen and morbid. But on this evening she has left the gay feast (l. 52) and has come to him through the rain, has stirred up the fire, and then has laid aside her wet cloak and shawl and gloves and has untied her hat and let her damp hair fall, and then has sat down beside him and called him, but he wouldn't answer (l. 40). So she put his arm about her waist and then made her shoulder bare and put her yellow hair out of the way and made his cheek lie on her shoulder, her hair falling again over his face, she meantime murmuring how she loved him. This was too much for his distracted brain. He goes "out of his head." This moment is the fulfillment of everything to him, and the insane thought occurs to him that he can keep it perpetually so by killing her and keeping her there in that position. So he carries out the plan by twisting her long yellow hair into a string and strangling her with it. Only he finds that positions have to be reversed somewhat and his shoulder now supports her head. It is next morning when he tells about it (l. 84), but he has no sense that he has committed a crime. The only thing that bothers him is the possibility that she may have suffered, and he repeats that she felt no pain (ll. 66, 67). The last line of the poem, quoted by some as if so full of meaning, is nothing more nor less than an addition to show the shattered

condition of his mind — he wonders that God hasn't said anything about it.

2. This poem may not be a pleasant thing nor of comfort to any reader. But as a bit of literary art it is remarkable, to say the least. Its chief importance, however, is as a study comprehending much in little, in the line of abnormal psychology.

XV. MAY AND DEATH, p. 516

First published in *The Keepsake*, 1857. Then included in *Dramatis Personæ*, 1864.

1. The friend "Charles" in the poem is Browning's cousin James Silverthorne.

2. To read the poem, one would at first suppose that the matter involved was not simply the death of a man who had been a friend from childhood up, but rather a matter of desperate love between man and woman, so extreme are the statements. In stanza I, the poet wishes that, when his friend died, three-quarters of the delightful things of spring had died too, and, as far as he is concerned, he wouldn't mind if the other quarter had died also — nothing of the beauty of spring left. He rebukes himself in stanza II, and realizes that there are many who ought to have opportunity to enjoy what he and Charles enjoyed together. So, amending his wholesale wish in the succeeding stanzas, he is in favor of having the spring at its best for the sake of others, only he thinks they wouldn't miss one plant which was so much in the woods where he walked with Charles, if that grew no more again. That plant reminds him so of his friend's death that the spot of red on its leaves comes from his heart, that's all.

3. The plant referred to is the spotted persicaria, *Polygonum persicaria*, which has purple stains, varying in size and vividness, on its leaves.

4. The expression in the early part of the poem, so disproportionate to the grief which we would naturally expect in the poet at loss of his cousin and friend, is consistent with Browning's impulsive nature. So also is that at the end, as to how much the sight of this plant pains him.

V

SOME OF THE SHORT POEMS PUBLISHED AFTER MRS. BROWNING'S DEATH

I. Confessions, p. 516

Published in *Dramatis Personæ*, 1864.

1. The poem is very human and very "Browningesque." The man is dying, and the clergyman is by him with the conventional line of talk. But to the dying man life is good and the world is no vale of tears. Instead of being in a properly solemn frame of mind, he finds his memory running back to light and color in the days gone by, to stolen interviews with the girl he loved. His dying fancy makes up a picture of the scene from the curtain and the medicine bottles.

2. The poem is exceedingly refreshing. Moreover, it is full of the subtle thirst for life and love.

II. Prospice, pp. 516, 517

First printed in *The Atlantic Monthly*, June, 1864.[1] The poem appeared in Browning's volume *Dramatis Personæ* the same year.

1. The poem was written in the autumn of 1861, — the autumn following Mrs. Browning's death. It is out of the innermost of Browning's soul. He looks upon death as the climax, the best and crowning chance to prove

[1] Vol. XIII, p. 694. Cf. Dowden, *Robert Browning*, London, 1904, pp. 274, 275.

what he's made of, — one splendid consummate fight at the last, and then the peace, the light, and clasping Elizabeth Barrett Browning's soul — that will be enough.

2. The dramatic intensity of the poem should have a first place in speaking of it. The description of the near approach to the last struggle and of the coming of the calm after the struggle is very dramatic.

3. The following notes may not come amiss:

a. The title *Prospice* means *Look forward,* or strictly, *Look thou forward,* — imperative singular of the verb *prospicere.*

b. P. 516, l. 71, *to feel the fog in my throat* — one needs to spend a winter in England to appreciate this expression fully. It accurately describes the sensation you sometimes have in London or Oxford — you certainly *feel the fog* in your throat.

c. P. 517, l. 2, *the place,* the place where he must struggle with Death, — the whole being an old figure, the journey of life. When the time comes, he must approach the place where Death waits in the fog and mist and snow, where the storm is thickest. "The foe," "the Arch Fear" (chief Fear, greatest Fear), is Death, but there is no escape, the strong man must pass that way.

d. But Browning has no thought of escape nor of defeat. There stands between him and "the reward of it all" only "one fight more, the best and the last." *Guerdon* (l. 9), requital, reward.

e. He has no wish to die an easy painless death, *e.g.* to die in his sleep as so many wish. He would hate to have Death spare him — bandage his eyes and let him creep past (ll. 13, 14).

f. No, he wants to die splendidly in the fiercest struggle like the heroes of old. And if he hasn't suffered enough in his life, if he hasn't had enough of pain, darkness, and cold, let them pile it on now and he'll take it, so that the account will be square. He wants to endure "all that's coming to him." This is the meaning of "pay glad life's arrears of pain, darkness and cold."

g. "For sudden the worst turns the best to the brave," (but only *to the brave*). For "the black minute," the intensest of the strife, comes to an end, and he passes out on the other side of storm and night. And all the rage of the elements and the raving of fiend-voices around him "shall dwindle, shall blend," — note how they gradually die down and are transformed and then gradually come out again —

> "Shall change, shall become first a peace out of pain,
>   Then a light, then thy breast,
> O thou soul of my soul!"

And he cares not what comes after that — he can leave the rest with God:

> "I shall clasp thee again,
> And with God be the rest!"

4. You will look far before you find a finer piece of work than Browning's *Prospice*, in so few lines, with such dramatic power, such courage, such love, such confidence in Immortality. We suggest that you commit this poem to memory, whether you commit anything else of Browning's or not.

III. A FACE, p. 518

Published in *Dramatis Personæ*, 1864.

1. It is a girl's face as the poet would have it done on canvas. Both the drawing and the coloring are with care and artistic taste.

2. *Correggio*, born 1494, died 1534, eminent Italian painter.

IV. A LIKENESS, pp. 518, 519

Published in *Dramatis Personæ*, 1864.

1. *A Likeness* is a genial poem, the point being how
little a visitor knows the associations that go with things
he notices when he's calling. In describing how a visitor
acts toward these things and how he blunders and how
we "squirm," it is brisk and incisive.

a. The first example is a portrait hanging in a room where
tea is taken —

> "And the wife clinks tea-things under."

Her cousin's innocent remark as he looks at the portrait,
the wife's spiteful rejoinder, her cousin's further remark,
while her husband is extremely self-conscious and aware
of the discomfort of his corns! — all this is a pretty good
reflection of human nature.

b. The next example is a picture in a bachelor's quarters,
with all the things a sporty bachelor accumulates — including a cast of the fist of the boxer from whom he has
taken lessons, "the Tipton Slasher" [1] (a man known to
the history of fistic sport), playing-cards which have been
used to shoot at and are preserved as records of marks-
manship, a satin shoe (with a history!) irreverently used
for a cigar-case, the horns of a chamois shot in the Chablais
in Savoy, a print of Rarey (a famous horse-trainer, Cruiser
being probably one of his horses), and one of Sayers (a
real boxing champion), and a set of Rabelais in small
volumes. But the main thing that concerns us is that
there's also a portrait of some girl. The visitor guesses
it's Jane Lamb, and guesses wrong. His remarks are

---

[1] The parenthetical quotations with which Browning accompanies many
of the things mentioned are, of course, explanatory remarks by the owner of
the "spoils."

only in careless jest and exaggeration, but we can readily imagine how with every word he's "getting in wrong."

c. The third example is an etching which the speaker owns. He tells, in a breezy way, of his friend's visit and of his emotions when the visitor admires this etching, and how he puts him off and presents him a piece of Volpato's (eminent engraver, 1738–1803). He realizes that if his visitor only knew — if he would only say the right thing to meet what he himself thinks in connection with the etching, he'd be so carried away he might give it to him, making a "bluff" that it is only a duplicate. *Marc Antonios*, etchings by the famous engraver Marc Antonio Raymondi (1487 or '88–1539). *Festina lentè*, literally *hasten slowly*, make haste slowly, *i.e.* "hold on."

2. The interest in the poem is not only literary but psychological.

V. Summum Bonum, p. 1295

Published in *Asolando*, Browning's last volume, which appeared on the day he died, Dec. 12, 1889. The remaining short poems discussed here were in the same volume.

1. *Summum Bonum* means the chief good, the greatest or ultimate good. It is a matter much discussed from classical times — what is the Summum Bonum?

2. Browning's poem is an intense love-poem, concentrating the excellence and beauty of things into the smallest compass and then putting forward something that beats all that, viz. love — the truth and trust

> "In the kiss of one girl."

3. "The bag of one bee" is, of course, the bag in which the bee carries the honey to his hive.

4. The poem is a good example of climax, everything in it culminating upon the last line,

> "In the kiss of one girl."

VI. SPECULATIVE, p. 1295

Published in *Asolando*, Dec. 12, 1889.

1. There's always speculation as to the question: If the personalities of human beings do endure beyond death, what are the conditions under which they exist? If, say, the good are in Heaven, what is that place or state like?

2. Browning answers that for him a piece of the old life on earth will be good enough, exactly as it was. It will be Heaven if only he and Mrs. Browning can meet and part no more.

3. It seems as if the meaning of the lines would be plainer with a different punctuation. Yet as they stand no one will miss their meaning. The language is very condensed. The first stanza says that "others may need new life in Heaven" — everything new — Man with new mind, Nature with new light, Art with new opportunity and new fulfillment. In sharp contrast to all this desire for newness is Browning's prayer that past minutes of the earth may return and remain, that the old earth-life may come back ("enmesh us" — notice the word), even as it was before with him and Mrs. Browning. For the last lines are addressed to her, and this poem is out of the depths of Browning's love for her.

4. It is better not to begin to say what I think of this poem, lest I say too much. I do not want to say extreme things. The poem focuses in one point of light several of the fundamental thoughts which we see so often in Browning's writings. You will not find many things of ten lines quite equal to it in your rummaging the literatures of the world. Just for the sheer joy of going over the words again, here it is:

Others may need new life in Heaven —
  Man, Nature, Art — made new, assume !
Man with new mind old sense to leaven,
  Nature — new light to clear old gloom,
Art that breaks bounds, gets soaring-room.

I shall pray : "Fugitive as precious —
  Minutes which passed, — return, remain !
Let earth's old life once more enmesh us,
  You with old pleasure, me — old pain,
So we but meet nor part again !"

VII. REPHAN, pp. 1314, 1315

Published in the same volume with the two poems just discussed.

1. The matter of the poem is very akin to the centre of Browning's way of looking at things. His belief in the good of imperfection and the good of struggle makes him keenly sympathize with the being on whom all the perfection of the star of the god Rephan grows stale and cloying and who is stirred by a desire to struggle through failure, suffering, and sin toward higher things and is therefore told by a voice,

"Thou art past Rephan, thy place be Earth !"

2. Browning himself says in a note (printed at bottom of first column, p. 1314) that the poem was "suggested by a very early recollection of a prose story by the noble woman and imaginative writer, Jane Taylor, of Norwich." As Dr. Berdoe [1] and the editors of the Globe Edition point out, Jane Taylor lived at Ongar, not Norwich. Her story was entitled *How it Strikes a Stranger* and was in vol. I of her work entitled *The Contributions of Q. Q.* Naturally enough, Browning's poem bears very little resemblance to Jane

[1] *Browning Cyclopædia*, ed. 1912, p. 383.

Taylor's story which he recalled across so many years. He got from it only the word Rephan and a suggestion.

VIII. REVERIE, pp. 1315–1317

Published in the same volume as the preceding.

1. The poem is a Confession of Faith that somewhere, sometime, we shall come to self-fulfillment in harmony with the universe, — strong buoyant faith that when rightly seen Power and Love are one.

a. The life of the race is repeated in epitome in the life of the individual. Therefore, the life of the individual and the life of the race shall both find fulfillment according to the same law : [1]

> "I for my race and me
>   Shall apprehend life's law:
> In the legend of man shall see
>   Writ large what small I saw
> In my life's tale: both agree."

b. Naturally progress will be from near to far, from within outward, — this is the key to the fulfillment : [2]

> "How but from near to far
>   Should knowledge proceed, increase?
> Try the clod ere test the star !
>   Bring our inside strife to peace
> Ere we wage, on the outside, war !"

So he looks into his own life which has been lived in the presence of infinite Power which seems at strife with Love.

c. Anyway, life is a great becoming, a splendid adventure : [3]

> "Then life is — to wake not sleep,
>   Rise and not rest, but press
> From earth's level where blindly creep
>   Things perfected, more or less,
> To the heaven's height, far and steep."

[1] P. 1315, ll. 74–78. [2] P. 1315, ll. 84–88. [3] P. 1317, ll. 53–57.

d. And Browning believes that, although Power in the universe is so evident and Love dimly shown, yet at last we shall find that "Power is Love:" [1]

> "I have faith such end shall be:
>   From the first, Power was — I knew.
> Life has made clear to me
>   That, strive but for closer view,
> Love were as plain to see."

2. The poem opens and closes with the same high note, that "there shall dawn a day," no matter when, no matter where — a day when Power shall have its way in him and he will find life's fulfillment.

IX. EPILOGUE, p. 1317

This is the Epilogue to *Asolando*, the volume published the day Browning died.

1. It has been well said that even if Browning had known that these were to be his last words to the world, he could not have given a more intimate and more vital message than in *Reverie* and in this *Epilogue*.

2. The *Epilogue* especially is a pointblank confession of what he is and how he wishes to be esteemed.   When he is dead, people will very likely mistake him, as is usually the case.   How will his friends think of him, when they are thinking in the night?   Are they going to think of him as lying low, imprisoned by Death, and pity him?   In life he was none of " the slothful, the mawkish, the unmanly " — he was not like " the aimless, helpless, hopeless."   Nay rather, he was

> "One who never turned his back but marched breast forward,
>   Never doubted clouds would break,

[1] P. 1317, ll. 63–67.

Never dreamed, though right were worsted, wrong would triumph,
Held we fall to rise, are baffled to fight better,
      Sleep to wake."

And he wants them to think of him "in the bustle of man's worktime," as not dead but alive, — struggling and progressing in the unseen world as he did here. Notice the contrast between thinking of him "at the midnight" and "at noonday," in the "sleeptime" and in the "worktime."

3. A word is needed as to the last stanza: "the unseen" to be greeted with a cheer is Browning after death. This is plain from the pronoun "him" which refers to "the unseen." "Breast and back as either should be," breast and back each in its place, not with breast where back should be, *i.e.* not turned to retreat. "Strive and thrive! . . . Speed, — fight on etc." all after *cry*.

4. The poem is quite beyond praise. It has too much reality in it to be subject to treatment as literature. It provokes the finest admiration for the man who wrote it. One evening just before his last illness Browning was reading the proofs of *Asolando* with his sister and daughter-in-law. And when he read the third stanza of the Epilogue, he stopped and said: "It almost looks like bragging to say this, and as if I ought to cancel it; but it's the simple truth; and as it's true, it shall stand." [1] It will be a sad day for any of us when we do not feel like bowing in the presence of such a personality as speaks through this Epilogue.

[1] Substance of incident related in the *Pall Mall Gazette* of Feb. 1, 1890. Browning's words are quoted exactly as reprinted from the *Gazette* by Berdoe, *Browning Cyclopædia*, ed. 1912, pp. 153, 154.

VI

THREE OF THE LONGER POEMS NOW STANDING AMONG THE DRAMATIC ROMANCES

THOUGH now standing under the head of *Dramatic Romances*, no one of these three poems was originally published in *Dramatic Romances and Lyrics* of 1845.[1]

I. THE PIED PIPER OF HAMELIN, pp. 353-356

Published in *Dramatic Lyrics*, 1842.

1. Its subtitle is *A Child's Story*, and there is added *Written for, and inscribed to, W. M. the Younger, i.e.* written for William Macready, Jr., son of the great actor William Macready.

2. People who think Browning is so hard have never read *The Pied Piper of Hamelin*, or, if they've read it, don't know it is Browning's. Children read it and enjoy it hugely, know it by heart and repeat it with gusto.[2] But when I say, "Well, Browning's not so hard — see how the children enjoy his *Pied Piper*," then comes the exclamation, "Oh! did Browning write *The Pied Piper*?"

3. A few notes:

a. *Pied*, variegated with spots of different colors. See description of his coat (v) and his scarf (vi).

b. *Hamelin* (German *Hameln*) is a town of 20,000 people (1905), in the province of Hanover, 33 miles by

[1] See explanation at the beginning of Chapter IV.
[2] It has been a pleasure to the writer to hear it. No doubt some of the children of the reader's acquaintance can repeat it.

the railroad southwest of the city of Hanover, in Prussia. It is situated on the river Weser, at the point where the Hamel flows in. Browning is mistaken when he says,

"Hamelin Town's in Brunswick."

It is not far from the borders of Brunswick and has been at times in its history under the protection of the dukes of Brunswick, but it is in Hanover.

c. The legend is found in various works, *e.g.* (1) Richard Verstegen, *Restitution of Decayed Intelligence in Antiquities concerning the English Nation*, 1605,[1] (2) Nathaniel Wanley, *The Wonders of the Little World, or a General History of Man*, 1678.[2]

d. A piper named Bunting, for the promise of a sum of money, freed the town from rats, by playing on his pipe while they followed until he led them into the Weser and they were drowned. The townsmen then refused to pay him. So he went away again, playing, followed by the children, 130 in all. He led them to a hill called the Koppelberg (or Koppenberg, as some spell it) whose side opened and they entered and disappeared. The event is recorded in inscriptions in the town, and was long regarded as historical. "For a considerable time the town dated its public documents from the event."[3]

e. The year was 1284 (June 26). Browning has July 22, 1376 (p. 356, ll. 31–33). How he got the date wrong by almost 100 years, no one seems to explain.

[1] Published, Antwerp, 1605; reprinted, London, 1673. Its author's real name was Richard Rowlands and he was born near the Tower of London, but many of his works were published under the name or initials of Richard Verstegen.

[2] Also eds. 1774, with revision and index, 1806–07, 2 vols., with additions by Wm. Johnston.

[3] *Encyclopædia Britannica*, 11th ed., Cambridge, 1910, vol. XII, p. 876, art. *Hameln*.

f. The town of Brandenburg, some 37 miles southwest of Berlin, and the town of Lorch in Würtemberg have tales of such an event as having taken place at each of them. There are similar Persian and Chinese legends. We recognize a widely diffused legend, fastened upon different localities.[1]

g. P. 354, l. 35, *Cham*, now usually written *khan*, — word for prince, chief, governor — here used for the head ruler of Tartary.

l. 37, *Nizam* (*Nizam-ul-Mulk*, Regulator of the State), the title of the native sovereigns who, since 1719, have ruled Hyderabad, an extensive territory in the interior of southern India. The territory is often called Nizam's Dominions.

4. The versification of the poem is rapid and full of variety. There are many of those grotesque rhymes with which Browning likes to decorate his humorous pieces. The drollest of them are: "Trump of Doom's tone" and "painted tombstone" (p. 354, ll. 14, 15), "river Weser" and "Julius Cæsar" (ll. 67, 69), "pickle-tub-boards" and "conserve-cupboards" (ll. 77, 78), "by psaltery" and "drysaltery" (ll. 82, 84), "rare havoc" and "Vin-de-Grave, Hock"[2] (p. 355, ll. 5, 6).

5. The humor is very rich. It is all so good that it seems out of order to quote a sample, but the Mayor's eye is perhaps a little better than any of the other droll descriptions:

> "Nor brighter was his eye, nor moister
> Than a too-long-opened oyster."[3]

---

[1] Some trace the origin of the legend to the Children's Crusade of 1212. This might be the thing which led to the legend's being adapted and attached to various places in Germany, but not the origin of the legend itself. In favor of there being some basis of fact in the case of Hameln, the article in the *Encyclopædia Britannica* points out that the Koppelberg is not one of the imposing elevations by which the town is surrounded, but a low hill barely enough to hide the children from sight as they left the town.

[2] Two kinds of wine arrayed at the end of the list, to make the rhyme.

[3] P. 353, ll. 90, 91.

II. The Statue and the Bust, pp. 372-375

Published in vol. I of *Men and Women*, 1855.

1. In the Piazza dell' Annunziata in Florence stands an equestrian statue of Grand Duke Ferdinand I (Ferdinand de' Medici, born about 1549, succeeded his brother Francesco I as Grand Duke of Tuscany in 1587, died 1609. He was a younger son of Cosimo the Great, 1519–1574). The statue is by the great sculptor John of Douay [1] (1524–1608), one of his finest works. It faces the *old* Riccardi Palace, now called the Antinori Palace. This is, of course, the palace mentioned in the first line of the poem and was where the Riccardi lived whose bride looked out and saw Duke Ferdinand ride by. It should not be confused with the palace (p. 372, ll. 54–74, especially ll. 57–62) [2] in the Via Larga (now called the Via Cavour), where the feast was held that night, at which the bridal pair were guests. (Lines 63–71 describe the Duke receiving them.) That was Duke Ferdinand's own residence.

2. The story is that Ferdinand had the statue so placed because in that palace of the Riccardi lived the lady he loved, kept a prisoner by a jealous husband.

3. The bust seems to be Browning's invention. He admits there's none there now (p. 374, l. 48).

4. The *crime* (p. 372, l. 59) was the usurpation of the authority of the Republic by Cosimo de' Medici (Cosimo the Elder, 1389–1464), referred to in lines 61 and 62 as the murder of the Republic. *Robbia's craft* (p. 374, l. 28, cf. l. 46), the kind of work in enamelled terra-cotta origi-

---

[1] P. 374, l. 61. He is usually called Giovanni da Bologna, John of Bologna.

[2] That was the Medici Palace and was sold in 1659 to the Riccardi, and so is now called the Riccardi Palace. But in the days of Ferdinand I, of course, the Medici lived there and the Riccardi lived in what was then the Palazzo Riccardi, viz. the palace toward which this statue faces.

nated by Luca della Robbia (who died in 1463) and carried on by the family for a hundred years. The last well-known artist of the family, Girolamo della Robbia, died in 1566. In the last line, *De te, fabula!* literally, *concerning thee, the story! i.e.* the story is concerning you, it hits your case, there's a moral in it for you.

5. The verse-form is *Terza Rima*, which originated with the Troubadours, and was first extensively used by Dante (1265–1321) in the *Divine Comedy* and to some extent by Boccaccio (1313–1375) after him. It was introduced into England by Sir Thomas Wyatt (1503–1542) or by the Earl of Surrey (1516–1547, their poems published together in Tottel's *Miscellany*, 1557), and has been variously adapted and experimented with by Sir Philip Sidney, Samuel Daniel, Lord Byron, and others. Mrs. Browning has used it for her *Casa Guidi Windows*. The finest piece of *Terza Rima* in English is Shelley's *Ode to the West Wind*. Browning does not handle it nearly so well as Shelley.

6. The point in this poem has been already referred to in our discussion of Browning's characteristics. The Duke and Riccardi's wife had decided to elope, to commit the sin. According to the teaching of Jesus (Matt. 5 : 27, 28), they were already guilty of it, having formed the purpose in their thoughts. But instead of carrying it out, they delayed days, weeks, years, still cherishing those desires. And their souls shrivelled. They were put to the test and failed. It tested them as surely as if it had been a good thing they delayed to do. Whatever has become of them, Browning is sure they do not see God nor have any place with those who "have dared and done :"

> "Only they see not God, I know,
> Nor all that chivalry of his,

> The soldier-saints who, row on row,
> Burn upward each to his point of bliss
> Since, the end of life being manifest,
> He had burned his way thro' the world to this." [1]

III. "CHILDE ROLAND TO THE DARK TOWER CAME," pp. 375-378

Published in vol. I of *Men and Women*, 1855.

1. This poem was written in Paris in one day, Jan. 3, 1852, and was not revised after that.

2. It was suggested, as Browning's note at the head of the poem indicates, by a line of Edgar's song in Shakespeare's *King Lear*.

a. As you remember, Edgar, to save his life, is disguised as a madman and acts the part. Pouring out a mass of incoherent nonsense in Act III scene IV, he sings at the end of the scene this snatch of a song:

> "Child Rowland to the dark tower came,
> His word was still, — Fie, foh, and fum,
> I smell the blood of a British man."

The great dissimilarity between the first line and what follows has suggested to several critics that Edgar, in his pretending to be crack-brained, throws together bits of two different songs. This is probably the case. The first line is evidently from a ballad older than Shakespeare's time and probably familiar to his audience, but it has not yet been elsewhere discovered. Traces of the other two lines, or rather of the "Fie, foh, and fum, etc.," have been found.[2]

[1] P. 374, ll. 79-84.
[2] See Furness, Variorum Shakespeare, *King Lear*, Philadelphia, 1880, pp. 201, 202 (same pp. in 10th ed. 1908). In spelling *Child Rowland* most editors follow the early editions, but I have seen one or two recent editions with the spelling *Childe Roland*.

b. The first line of Edgar's song caught Browning's imagination. Undoubtedly what struck Browning was the word "came" — *arrived, accomplished what he set out to do*. This chimed in with Browning's nature and his doctrine of sticking, with iron determination, to what you undertake. So he let his fancy loose on conditions preceding and attending the knight's arrival at the Tower.

c. Browning's poem, then, should be weaned entirely from Shakespeare's *King Lear* and Edgar's pretended madness, except for the slightest contact, viz. this: the line of an old song in Edgar's mouth fired Browning's imagination.

d. "Child," when used as in this song (and generally spelled *Childe* when so used), was applied to young knights and young men of noble birth. See Spenser's use of it in *The Faerie Queene*. Cf. Byron's styling himself "Childe Harold" in *Childe Harold's Pilgrimage*.

3. "Childe Roland" is Sir Roland, the strongest and bravest of Charlemagne's paladins.

a. Charlemagne (*Charles, the Great*), King of the Franks, was crowned Emperor of the Holy Roman Empire, in St. Peter's Church in Rome, on Christmas day, in the year 800.

b. Around him and his knights has grown up a mass of legend, (as around King Arthur and his knights, only with very much more historical basis).

c. Most famous of all Charlemagne's knights is Roland, who commanded the rear guard of the army in the retreat from Spain in the year 778 and, when the rear guard was cut off, lost his life in battle at Roncesvalles (French, *Roncevaux*), in Navarre. So much is historical. The legends gathering about the event have made an epic, the famous *Chanson de Roland*, or Song of Roland, preserved in Old French, — immensely enlarging, of course, his actual prowess.

d. The adventure referred to in the ballad from which Edgar sings a scrap is some one of the other legends which became attached to the name of Roland — some adventure of his earlier years, the quest of the Dark Tower.

4. Browning's poem has to be considered entirely apart from any historical basis. It is sheer imagination. The poem is in the mouth of the knight whose adventure is related. It is therefore reasonable to suppose that Browning meant to imply that the adventure came to a successful issue, for if reaching the Dark Tower brought him into something which was the last of him, how could he be relating thus much of what befell him? We get the impression from the poem that it is some time afterward, perhaps years after, that Roland is relating how he finally reached the Tower. He does not go on with any account of what happened after he blew his horn. "That," as Kipling would say, "is another story." The thing on which Browning's imagination works is simply the last afternoon of the journey and the arrival before the Tower. The earlier wandering is referred to, but only because of its bearing on this last afternoon.

5. The circumstances are quite plain :

a. The quest of the Dark Tower was a quest to which knights, one generation after another, had devoted themselves (stanzas VII, XXXIII, XXXIV). (For a famous example of such quests, compare the quest of the Holy Grail.)

b. There existed some information as to the general marks of the region in which the Tower was situated and a description of the immediate surroundings of the Tower (stanza III, stanza XXX), also a description of the Tower itself by which it could be recognized (stanza XXXI). But the *direction* in which to search seems to have been lost, for the knight in the present adventure had wandered world-wide (stanza IV).

c. Knights who devoted themselves to the quest of the Tower were called "the Band" (stanza VII), *i.e.* when a knight had sworn to take up this quest, he had joined "the Band."

d. Why some knights so devotedly gave themselves to this quest is not explained. The aspect of things as the poem closes would seem, however, to justify the idea that it was with purpose to avenge some great wrong. (We will discuss the close of the poem later.)

6. The following comment may be of use in reading the poem:

Stanza I —*on mine,* my eye — his eye watching the working of his lie on my eye; *pursed,* puckered up; *scored,* made notches in (derived from keeping the score by cutting notches in a stick); *one more victim,* Roland thinks this fellow's business is simply to send men astray.

Stanza II — *'gin write,* begin to write; *dusty thoroughfare,* the cripple sits at the edge of the travelled road, from which the knight turns off.

Stanza III — The knight has reached the region in which the Dark Tower is situated.

Stanza IV — *what with,* somewhat with, partly with (*what* used adverbially), — rather old-fashioned but still heard occasionally.

Stanzas V, VI, and VII are really all one sentence. There is no conclusion to the sentence until stanza VII. So there should be something other than a period at the end of stanza VI.

Stanza VI — *scarves* (plural of scarf), *staves* (plural of staff), to be used at the funeral, a part of the ceremony and display of the old days.

Stanza VIII — *its estray*, viz. the knight himself, now turned astray on the plain.

Stanza IX — *pledged to the plain*, having decided to travel the plain and having begun to do so, having committed himself to it.

Stanza X — *ignoble nature*, natural things of such poor quality; *cockle*, common name for several different weeds, growing in such a place as this it would be darnel (genus *Lolium*) or cockle-bur (genus *Xanthium*); *spurge*, harsh weeds of the genus *Euphorbia; treasure-trove*, money or other valuables found hidden in the earth or anywhere, the owner not being known, — talk about weeds' growing, a bur would have been like finding a treasure.

Stanza XI — *It nothing skills*, it makes no difference, there's no use trying; *calcine*, to convert into powder by heat or into a substance that can be readily crushed (for the idea of heat connected with the end of the world, see 2 Peter 3 : 10).

Stanza XII — *bents*, spears of stiff wiry grass; *pashing*, striking, crushing.

Stanza XIII — *devil's stud*, devil's stable, — *stud*, a collection of horses, also the place where they are kept.

Stanza XIV — *colloped neck*, a collop is a chunk of flesh, — this horse's neck is made up of bunches or lumps as if of collops put together, or as if an effort had been made to chop it up into collops.

Stanza XVI — *Not it*, it can't do what he expected of it (cf. preceding line).

Stanza XVII — *durst*, archaic for dared, still used to some extent; *faugh!* exclamation of disgust; *a parchment*, on which is written the crime for which he is hanged; *his*

own bands, the men who had supported him in his insur-
rection, bands of revolutionists or malcontents.

Stanza XVIII — *a howlet*, an owlet.

Stanza XIX — *bespate*, spattered; *spumes*, bits of foam
or froth.

Stanza XXI — *which*, the river.

Stanza XXII — *a plash*, puddle.

Stanza XXIII — *cirque*, circle; *mews*, enclosure, place of
confinement (plural of *mew*, a cage for hawks, a coop for
fowls); *brewage*, anything produced by brewing, a malt
drink as beer or ale.

Stanza XXIV — *furlong*, 40 rods, one-eighth of a mile;
Tophet's tool, tool from hell. Tophet was in the valley of
Hinnom, near Jerusalem, — the valley where the sewage
and filth of the city were dumped and where fires were
kept burning to consume offal and carcasses. In its earlier
history, this valley was a place of altars to Molech and of
abominable rites.[1] The Greek word *Gehenna* (the only
word in the New Testament which is properly translated
hell) is from the Hebrew *Ge-Hinnom*, valley of Hinnom.
Naturally enough, Tophet and Gehenna came to be sym-
bolic of torment or destruction.[2] The word Tophet is
not often heard in conversation among us except in such
expressions as "hotter than Tophet."

Stanza XXV — *stubbed*, covered with stubs, *i.e.* stumps
left from broken trees. The same piece of ground is
described in these three lines. Its history is plain from its
appearance: once it was a piece of woods, next it became

[1] See Jer. 7:31; 32:35; 2 Chron. 28:3; 33:6, and Josiah's action in
regard to the matter 2 Kings 23:10.

[2] Cf. Milton, *Paradise Lost*, Bk. I, ll. 404, 405:

> "The pleasant valley of Hinnom, Tophet thence
> And black Gehenna called, the type of hell."

a marsh, and now it is "mere earth desperate and done with." The same ground is described in the last two lines of this stanza : *within a rood*, a quarter of an acre ; *rubble*, rough broken stones.

Stanza XXVII — *Apollyon*, the angel of the bottomless pit (Rev. 9 : 11) ; *dragon-penned* (Latin *penna*, a feather), having feathers like those on a dragon's wing. Cf., in *The Ring and the Book :* [1]

"Twitch out five pens where plucking one would serve."

Stanza XXVIII — *with such name to grace*, if one may call the "ugly heights and heaps" by such a name as mountains.

Stanza XXX — *scalped mountain*, mountain having a bare top, like the head of a man who has been scalped by an Indian ; *nonce*, the once, the one occasion, (chiefly in *for the nonce*), — *at the very nonce*, at the very moment, at the critical moment.

Stanza XXXII — *Not see?* repeating someone's suggestion or a thought which he knows may be in his listeners' minds : "Maybe it was getting so dark that you couldn't see the Tower until you were almost on it ;" *heft*, same as *haft* (both from O. E. *hæft*), hilt, handle.

Stanza XXXIII — *Not hear?* similar to *not see?* in stanza XXXII.

Stanza XXXIV — *slug-horn:* What Browning has in mind is a short crude sort of bugle, but the word *slug-horn* is really a corruption of *slogan*, rallying-cry, and the use of it (older than Browning) as if it signified a *horn* is entirely erroneous. Wright's *English Dialect Dictionary* has "*slug-horn*, a short and ill-formed horn of an animal of the ox kind, turned downwards and stunted in growth,"

[1] *Count Guido Franceschini*, p. 736, l. 17.

and one might argue that *slug-horn* to blow on is that word, with a history similar to the use of *horn*. But the use of *slug-horn* for *slogan* (with no sense of horn) shows plainly that such use as Browning's here is a mistake. The punctuation which places anything except a period after *blew* in the last line is surely wrong and is prompted by a misinterpretation. "Childe Roland to the Dark Tower came" is not what he blew, but simply a summing up of the adventure, up to this point. Of course, in a certain sense that blast on the horn was a summing up of the adventure, and in that sense only can it be argued that the horn seemed to say, "Childe Roland to the Dark Tower came."

7. The account, then, which the knight gives of his reaching the Tower:

The knight relates that he had been for years on this quest, in a "whole world-wide wandering," and now his hope had "dwindled into a ghost," when he came to where by the highway sat a repulsive cripple. The knight evidently had long ago lost his horse, for now he was on foot. Exhausted and discouraged, he asked the cripple the way to the Dark Tower, and the cripple indicated that it was in yonder ominous tract of country. The knight, nothing doubting that the cripple was lying, in fact was posted there to misdirect travellers and get them into trouble, nevertheless turned as directed. He had not hope enough left to bear the "obstreperous joy success would bring." He does not care what comes next, only if there can be some end. He will go on and become one of that glorious company who have given themselves to this quest and have failed. He is like a sick man very near to death, who seems indeed dead and hears them speak of him as dead and hears the discussion of details about his funeral, and desires only that he may not come out of his trance and embarrass them. So this knight has so long been counted one of "the Band" devoted to the quest of the Dark Tower, so long has it been prophesied that he will fail, that just to fail like the rest seems the best thing he can do. The only question with him is whether he is fit to join that company of those who, in spite of all high endeavor, failed.

And so he turns, "quiet as despair," into the path across the dreary plain. The desolation is great, even at first, and increases in repulsiveness as he goes on. The sun of the late afternoon shoots out a "grim red leer" at him. He loses sight of the highway whence he came, and could not go back. There is nothing to do but to go on. The plain is so barren that a bur on it would be finding a treasure. Nature seems to have given up as impossible making anything of this place. As he goes on, there are some thistle-stalks with chopped heads, some dry wiry grass, some dock-leaves all bruised up, — the whole as if trampled by a brute's hoofs. Further on, he comes where the ground has been flooded and now is left covered with a coating of mud which looks as if it were "kneaded up with blood" underneath and through which the thin dry blades of grass prick up "as scant as hair in leprosy." The only living creature in sight is a ghastly specimen of a horse, fit only to be turned out of the devil's stables as of no further use.

So repulsive is everything external that the knight tries to get courage from his own heart by thinking of other days and his valiant friends. "One taste of the old time sets all to rights," — will help him now in spite of what is around him. So he thinks of Cuthbert, handsome fellow, and his affectionate way, — until he comes to Cuthbert's disgrace — one night, whatever it was he did, shattered the confidence and friendship. There is no comfort nor encouragement in thinking of Cuthbert. Well then, think of Giles, he was "the soul of honor." Think of him as standing there just as he stood ten years ago when knighted. A brave man and honorable, "What honest man should dare (he said) he durst." But just here the encouragement that was arising from thinking of Giles is dispelled by Giles' end : some revolt Giles had headed, some outlawry, — and the mental picture of the brave young fellow turns to the picture of him hanged as a criminal. And so it goes on — no comfort in memories, as Roland plods on. He finds no encouragement within himself, and he brings his mind back to "this present," this dismal plain, on which the presence of an owlet or a bat would be something to be appreciated.

He has gone on, thinking, not noticing much his surroundings for a while, and now is surprised by coming upon a little river flowing across the plain, not sluggishly as would seem fitting to the place (you see, he has drawn nearer the hills without noticing it and there is more reason for current than he supposes), but frothing and foaming spitefully as if fit for the hot hoof of the devil. There are alders and willows on its banks and dipping into it. The knight wades through, reaching his spear ahead of him to find holes and avoid getting in too deep. So gruesome is the whole thing, that he would not be surprised to find his spear tangled in a dead man's hair or beard, or even to set his foot upon a dead man's face. Once, when spearing ahead of himself thus, something cried or squealed, which he rigidly makes himself understand was probably a water-rat struck by his spear, but to his overwrought nerves it seemed for the moment a baby's shriek.

Reaching the other bank of the river, he thinks for a

moment that it may prove better, but is disappointed. If possible, its grotesque hideousness exceeds what he saw before. And its hideousness is of another sort, showing evidence of human or fiendish cruelty: an awful struggle of some sort, human or bestial, has taken place, and passing by the marks of that, he comes to a torture-machine. Further on, he comes to land "desperate and done with," and then to soil that is revolting to look on and to the one tree, a "palsied oak" which has a grinning cleft in it. This is all wearing hard on the man, exhausted as he is with wanderings and hardships.

His eyes fixed on the hideousness immediately around him, he is convinced that he is arriving nowhere, that there is naught to point his footstep further. The thought has hardly formed itself in his mind, when he feels his cap brushed by the wing of a great black bird who looks as if he might be "Apollyon's bosom-friend." Looking up and after the bird, the knight perceives that he is among the hills, or mountains if you may call them so. He is surprised at how they have stolen upon him, the fact being, of course, that he has been so absorbed in the desolation and the repulsive sights near at hand and so absorbed in his own thoughts that he has walked into the hilly part, not noticing it in the dusk of evening. He does not see how to get clear of these hills now (he has no idea of turning back). But his mind is working as a mind does when half-recognizing something without conscious effort. What his mind is working over is the marks for identifying the location of the Dark Tower, coupling these that he has held in memory for years with what the eye takes in from these hills. Suddenly, with a flush of heat over his whole body, the realization comes upon him that this is the place he has been seeking. With that, instantly he recognizes the marks, the two hills on the right like two bulls crouching with locked horns, and the "tall scalped mountain" on the left, — and in the middle the Dark Tower itself, answering exactly to the description treasured in the mind of every knight who has sought it. It must be the one, there is no other like it in the world. The recognition of the whole thing has come to him as he was almost running upon it, just as a sailor gets no warning of an unseen reef until his ship strikes it. To the suggestion that he didn't see because of the gathering darkness and so came close to the Tower before knowing it was there, the knight answers that the sunset kindled up again [1] "through a cleft" in the hills (or perhaps a cleft in the clouds). And as that sunset brightened and showed him the scene, there lay the hills like giants at a hunting when the game is cornered and they look on to see the death — "Now stab and end the creature" — only, in this case the knight himself being the creature in such desperate straits. Someone suggests that maybe he didn't hear anything to attract his attention. To this the knight answers that "noise was everywhere." This was, of course, the noise in his own brain, the turmoil of the realization that he had reached what so many worthier than he had sought in vain. The tremendous excitement and nervous tension which came with that realization make him seem to hear tolled in his ears the names of all the lost adventurers who have gone on this quest, with praise of each one's strength and prowess, and success in other endeavors, — yet each was "lost, lost!" Of course, it is the history of the quest, brooded over so much, now rushing through his mind. It seems to him as if this moment, tolling the names of

[1] The writer has several times seen sunsets die down and then kindle again so that they were very much brighter 15 or 20 minutes later.

those knights and their fate, knells "the woe of years." And in the tremendous tension and excitement of the moment, not only does he seem to hear their names and their fate tolled in his ears, but his heightened imagination pictures them all as ranged along the hills ("There they stood," — *they* being the lost adventurers), looking at him now, at him who has reached the Tower, to see how he will conclude the quest, — grimly he puts it "to view the last of me," *i.e.* to see how he will behave himself in the last struggle, which he thinks will very likely cost him all. They form in his imagination "a living frame for one more picture" ("living frame" in apposition with "they . . . ranged along the hill-sides"). The "one more picture" is to be the knight himself doing what he is about to do, the picture of what's going to happen when he blows his horn. How great the strain and how heightened his imagination may be judged from the fact that he not only sees the adventurers lost on this quest watching what he will do, but it is "in a sheet of flame" he sees them and knows them all. And yet, under such circumstances, exhausted as he is and with all those of the past who have tried and failed looking down upon him, with all that may come to pass in the next minute, *dauntless he sets the slug-horn to his lips and blows.*

"What happened then?" is the question so many ask. Why, but one thing could happen. Sir Roland has sought so long, and now has found the Tower and *will do what he came to do.* That blast on his horn is *a challenge,* — not simply a blast blown to celebrate his having found the Tower. The setting for the whole — those faces along the hillsides "a living frame" — for what? For the picture of the battle which takes place when, in answer to his horn, the inhabitants of the Tower rush out on him. He is "dauntless" — in view of what? Dauntlessly faces what's going to happen the next minute after he sets that horn to his lips. Exhausted in body, worn and harassed in soul, with a consciousness of all that is at stake, he does not delay nor hesitate, but dauntless blows his challenge. This is exactly in the spirit of Robert Browning. But to tell what comes after would be "another story." Browning started to describe Roland's reaching the Dark Tower. And having seen him reach it, Browning leaves the story with the simple summary which started him to writing it: "*Childe Roland to the Dark Tower Came.*"

8. The poem as a work of art:

a. The poem is fascinating. This fascination is due to (1) the wonderful descriptions in it, (2) the constant sense that the story corresponds to something in our lives, and (3) the desperate determination and perseverance of the knight.

b. The poem contains many stanzas of exquisite poetry, and some stanzas which cannot by any stretching of the word be said to be poetry at all. (1) To justify our remark as to exquisite poetry, we have only to cite such phrases as (in stanza IV)

"my hope
Dwindled into a ghost not fit to cope
With the obstreperous joy success would bring,"

the details of the simile wrought out in stanzas V, VI, and VII, the "quiet as despair" in stanza VIII, the whole of stanza XV, the lines in stanza XX

"Low scrubby alders kneeled down over it;
Drenched willows flung them headlong in a fit
Of mute despair,"

and those in stanza XXVII

"And just as far as ever from the end!
Nought in the distance but the evening, nought
To point my footstep further!"

and in stanza XXX

> "Burningly it came on me all at once,
> This was the place!"

and the whole of stanzas XXXII, XXXIII, and XXXIV. (2) To justify the other part of the remark, *i.e.* as to the unpoetic passages in the poem, we need only appeal to such a weak and ineffective line as that at the end of stanza XIV,

> "He must be wicked to deserve such pain,"

very evidently put in simply to finish out the stanza, and to such things as, in stanza XXI,

> "It may have been a water-rat I speared,
> But, ugh! it sounded like a baby's shriek,"

and in stanza XXII,

> "Toads in a poisoned tank,
> Or wild cats in a red-hot iron cage."

This last example is an extreme one, — bare, realistic, with no touch of idealism. And without idealism there is no art of any kind — no poetry, of course. There are many other passages in the poem not so extreme as this but belonging in the same category. In stanza XIII we read

> "As for the grass, it grew as scant as hair
> In leprosy,"

and in stanza XXVI,

> "Now patches where some leanness of the soil's
> Broke into moss or substances like boils."

These are almost as extreme and as lacking in any possible claim to be considered poetry. (3) It should be added, however, that these extremely realistic descriptions do, whether poetry or not, accomplish what Browning wanted to do, viz. give us a vivid sense of the repulsiveness and hideousness of the plain over which the knight goes.[1]

9. The poem would well repay study from the standpoint of psychology. The working of the exhausted knight's mind, in view of the whole situation as he starts across the plain, is interesting, and especially the state of mind he has gotten into by the time he fords the river. But still more significant is his account of his experience before the Tower. Natural enough is the fact that the crucial moment brings vividly before his mind the whole history of the quest, — a phenomenon to be classed with that reported of persons drowning, that sometimes a man's whole life rushes past his mind's eye in a brief space of time.

10. What did Browning mean by the poem?

a. First of all he meant to write a piece of dramatic narrative, and he certainly did it. Anyone who reads the poem a few times will not soon forget it.

b. And Browning did *not* mean a detailed allegory. All such interpretations are unjustifiable. Browning's own statement made to Dr. F. J. Furnivall[2] was that the poem is not an allegory. Nothing could be more absurd and further from Browning's poem than Dr. Berdoe's undertaking to say[3] that it is "a picture of the Age of

[1] To the remark as to the unpoetic passages in "*Childe Roland*," Prof. Charles B. Wright and Mrs. John H. McCrackan have, in conversation with me, made strong objections. Prof. Wright's argument is that the passages cited as unpoetic are necessary to the artistic effect of the whole, and that therefore the poem as an artistic unit justifies these passages, and that it is unjust to isolate them and say that they are lacking in poetic art. Mrs. McCrackan's argument is that these passages represent sublimated hideousness, and that this is as truly a form of idealism as is sublimated beauty, and that therefore these are examples of poetic art. Both these arguments should be given due weight in connection with the above paragraph.

[2] The London Browning Society's *Papers*, Part III, p. 21, quoted by Berdoe, *Browning Cyclopædia*, ed. 1912, p. 103.

[3] Berdoe, *Browning Cyclopædia*, pp. 104, 105.

Materialistic Science," [1] and in particular a condemnation of medical research by means of inoculating lower animals.[2] Nor is the blast of the horn "a warning to others." [3]   All the best words in the last stanza lose their meaning unless the blowing of the horn is a defiance. (See our discussion earlier in this lecture.)

c. But Browning is not a man who could put forward a thing so graphic and stirring as this without some meaning below the mere words. And the meaning is plain: it is *unfaltering loyalty to an ideal*. (Read Prof. Royce's *Philosophy of Loyalty* and see how loyalty to something, anything, gives life a meaning.) Unfaltering loyalty to an ideal and iron determination to do what we undertake to do — these will carry us through. The desperate tenacity of the knight in going on and the desperate valor, no matter how extreme his exhaustion, at the end — these are of the soul of Robert Browning.

d. While the poem, then, is in no sense an allegory, it is a vivid story of a man's sticking to his quest in the midst of all dismal and repulsive surroundings and meeting the climax of hardship and suffering undismayed. It is very like human life at its hardest and blackest, — nothing to cheer us inside or outside of ourselves — nothing to do but to face it grimly and go on — and like enough on top of all that is hard and dismal will come the most desperate struggle — yet to meet it with a dauntless soul. That is what is in Childe Roland's coming to the Dark Tower.

[1] Called by Berdoe, p. 105, also "Atheistic Science."
[2] This latter part Berdoe hangs upon the words,

> "Toads in a poisoned tank,
> Or wild cats in a red-hot iron cage."

It seems to be inoculation rather than vivisection he means by phrases "gloat over their animal victims" and "experimental torturer."
[3] Berdoe, *Browning Cyclopædia*, p. 105 end.

VII

FOUR OF THE MAJOR POEMS IN MEN AND WOMEN

THESE four poems were published in *Men and Women*, 2 vols., 1855, and still stand in that division of Browning's works. *An Epistle* and *Bishop Blougram's Apology* were originally in vol. I, *Cleon* and *One Word More* in vol. II.

I. AN EPISTLE CONTAINING THE STRANGE MEDICAL EXPERIENCE OF KARSHISH, THE ARAB PHYSICIAN, pp. 441-445

Browning had the rare ability to think outside of the atmosphere in which he lived, *i.e.* to set himself outside of Christian civilization, free himself from it to an unusual degree, and see how things look to one brought up in a different environment. This ability is much needed. In our estimate of pagan customs, *e.g.* the holding of gladiatorial shows in the arena, we are too quick. "Put yourself in his place" and see. In our estimate of other religions we need the same quality. A little realization of their point of view would save us from many an absurd snap-judgment. Browning's ability to do this is strikingly shown in several poems: *e.g.* in *Caliban upon Setebos*, a primitive intelligence trying to think out the mysteries of things; in *Cleon*, a Greek pagan poet and his attitude toward life and toward St. Paul's preaching of the Christian faith; but most strikingly of all in *An Epistle*.

1. In the eleventh chapter of the Fourth Gospel (usually called the Gospel according to St. John) is an account of

the death of Lazarus of Bethany, near Jerusalem, and his being raised from the dead by Jesus of Nazareth. That is all.

2. Now one of the strongest desires of humanity is to know something about what becomes of a man when he is dead. Is he extinct? If not, is he unconscious and will wake some day? Or is he conscious? If so, where is he? what does he see? what does he hear? what does he do? does he know what's taking place on earth? and so on.

3. Now, in the case of Lazarus, here was a man supposed to have lain dead four days. He could answer these questions, if he was really dead and raised to life again. Yet not a solitary syllable is related as to anything he said about his condition or experience between his death and his resurrection, nor how this affected his view of life. The questions have been asked thousands of times — everyone of you have heard some of them: How did he act? What did he say? How did life look to him?

4. Robert Browning is the only one I know of who has had the audacity to imagine how Lazarus acted and how he looked at life.[1] Browning has done it with great skill.

a. His observer is Karshish, an Arab physician, skilled in the science of the time. And Browning, with absolute consistency, does not impute to him any of the medical science of our time, but the medical science of centuries gone by, — with charms, queer dosage, and so on. The date is consistently laid just before the siege of Jerusalem which ended in its destruction in the year 70 A.D.[2]

[1] Browning does not undertake to imagine what Lazarus said about his experience while his body lay in the tomb, but somewhat of Lazarus' experience is implied in his estimate of values after his resurrection.

[2] P. 442, ll. 1–3; p. 444, ll. 10–14. The Jews revolted in 66 A.D. Vespasian began the siege of Jerusalem, but was made Emperor in 69, and his son Titus concluded the siege in the year 70.

b. The Arab physician is travelling for information — so common a way to learn when books were scarce — one of the best means of education anyway. He writes letters to an older physician named Abib, his teacher,[1] telling of his observations. This is now the twenty-second letter since he started on his travels:[2]

"And writeth now the twenty-second time."

c. With great naturalness his adventures and especially many curious observations, such as would be interesting to Abib, are woven in, — his hardships in travel, his being beaten by robbers, his being treated as a spy, his observation of fevers, epilepsy, scalp-disease, his information as to gums, herbs, charms, extract[3] of spiders, and so on. If Browning, from a sense of delicacy, had left out these, we'd have no such atmosphere of reality as hangs round this Arab doctor's letter. It is a source of considerable wonder that this effect can be produced. It is accomplished partly by the technical nature of the details given, partly by the touching on his adventures showing the troubled condition and dangers of the country, and partly by the informal style of the writing.

d. It soon becomes evident that Karshish has something on his mind which interests him more than these other professional observations. This finally comes out apologetically, and he frequently tries to switch off from it to his other observations, but cannot let it alone.

e. The thing that interests him is a case he has found here in Bethany, "one Lazarus a Jew,"[4] who believes that

---

[1] P. 441, ll. 66 sqq.   [2] P. 441, l. 78.

[3] When Karshish breaks off (p. 442, l. 23) it is not plain whether he meant to drop the spiders into wine (his most available form of anything alcoholic) and make a *tincture*, or boil them in water and make a *decoction*.

[4] P. 442, l. 83. The name is not given for some time after Karshish begins to tell of the case. This is in keeping with the informal style of his letter and also with his attitude toward this case.

he was dead and raised to life again. Karshish looks at the case from the medical standpoint — the medical science of his time: (1) He considers it "a case of mania — sub-induced by epilepsy." [1] (2) The one who brought him out of his trance was "a Nazarene physician of his tribe." [2] (3) This was accomplished

> "by the exhibition of some drug
> Or spell, exorcization, stroke of art," [3]

unknown to Karshish. (4) This Nazarene physician un-fortunately has been put to death many years ago at the instigation of a mob,[4] and so Karshish cannot talk the matter over with him.

So far, so good. No cause for reticence in writing of such a matter.

f. But that is not all. Karshish, in spite of himself, is interested in *Lazarus' way of looking at life.* Of this he cannot help giving some details,[5] and these are very striking.

g. But the thing he most hesitates to report is *Lazarus' view of his countryman* who, he believes, raised him from the dead. It seems to the man of science almost profane.[6] This Lazarus believes [7] that Jesus of Nazareth was God dwelling in human flesh, who bade him "Rise" and he did rise.

h. Karshish apologizes again for giving this case, throws

---

[1] P. 442, ll. 54–56.   [2] P. 442, l. 75.   [3] P. 442, ll. 57, 58.

[4] P. 444, ll. 33–49, especially ll. 37, 38. Karshish (ll. 42, 49) explains that the death of the Nazarene took place at the time of the earthquake and supposes that his inability to stop the earthquake was what brought to a climax the anger of the people against him. Cf. Karshish's own explana-tion of the portent of that earthquake (ll. 43–45) with the circumstances as related in Matt. 27: 50–53. Nothing could better show Browning's ability to keep the standpoint of his observer.

[5] P. 442, l. 82–p. 444, l. 32, the main part of the letter.

[6] P. 444, ll. 57, 58, 64.   [7] P. 444, ll. 51–67.

in a few other medical observations, explains the circumstances under which he met the man, and closes his letter.

i. Then in a postscript, the conception Lazarus has of Jesus burning in the physician's mind, the new world of thought opened by it staring him in the face, he adds the statement of what the Incarnation according to the terms stated by Lazarus would mean to mankind if it could be true, what it does mean if it is true : [1]

> "The very God ! think, Abib; dost thou think?
> So, the All-Great were the All-Loving too —
> So, through the thunder comes a human voice
> Saying, 'O heart I made, a heart beats here !
> Face, my hands fashioned, see it in myself !
> Thou hast no power nor mayst conceive of mine,
> But love I gave thee, with myself to love,
> And thou must love me who have died for thee !'"

5. *An Epistle* is altogether a remarkable piece of imagination, giving very truly (1) how Christ's deeds must have struck a man of education when he first came in contact with the report of them, and (2) how the claims made for him by his followers must have struck the educated men of those days outside of that circle.

[1] P. 445, ll. 1–8. Mayor's general remark should be quoted here, because he cites this passage as an illustration of the quality to which he refers. Joseph B. Mayor, *Chapters on English Metre*, 2d ed., Cambridge, 1901, pp. 217, 218 :

"I hardly know whether it is fancy or not, but to me there is no poetry which has such an instantaneous solemnizing power as that of Browning. We seem to be in the company of some rough rollicking Silenus, and all of a sudden the spirit descends upon him, the tone of his voice changes, and he pours out strains of sublimest prophecy. To use his own figure, a sudden breeze dispels the smoky haze of the crowded city, and in a moment we are conscious of the 'crystal silentness' of snow-crowned Alps towering over our heads. I will close with the concluding lines of a poem which has always seemed to me to have this effect in a remarkable degree, *The Strange Experience of Karshish, the Arab Physician*."

6. The point of the whole poem is too evident to need discussion :

a. We say we believe in things unseen and eternal. We say we believe that spiritual things are worth while and that material things are not of so great consequence. We say we believe this life is a part of an endless life and that death cannot destroy us. But do we live as if we believed these things?

b. Taking Lazarus, a man supposed to have seen behind the veil, and who therefore is taken as one who knows, *realizes*, all these things which we profess to believe, Browning shows how this man looks at life — how any man would look at life, if things unseen and eternal were actually real to him. This Lazarus has a different scale of values from that which most of us have. To Lazarus, things that so disturb others are of small consequence : the coming of a Roman army to destroy Jerusalem, the passing of a mule with a load of gourds — all the same to him.[1] Nothing is of consequence to him except what pertains to personality : a look from his child, showing something of the child's soul, stirs him deeply.[2] This Lazarus knows what eternal life means, and says [3]

> "he will wait patient to the last
> For that same death which must restore his being
> To equilibrium."

Knowing the reality of the unseen and eternal around the seen and transient,

> "He holds on firmly to some thread of life
> Which runs across some vast distracting orb
> Of glory on either side that meagre thread,
> Which, conscious of, he must not enter yet —
> The spiritual life around the earthly life." [4]

[1] P. 443, ll. 31–34.   [2] P. 443, ll. 34–50.
[3] P. 443, ll. 90–92.   His experience has done its work on his soul.
[4] P. 443, ll. 63, 65–68.

7. A few notes:

P. 441, ll. 59 sqq. The salutation is after the manner of Greek and Latin letters, familiar to us, but is confused a little by the large number of phrases arrayed in apposition. It runs: (l. 59) "Karshish . . . to Abib" (l. 65), and exactly parallel to that is (l. 73)

> "The vagrant Scholar to his Sage at home."

The verb of the first part of the paragraph, if any is needed, is "sends greeting" which appears in the second part. "Sends" governs also "three samples etc." The subject of "writeth" (l. 78) is "the vagrant Scholar."

l. 60, *not-incurious: curious*, having an inquiring mind, eager for knowledge — *incurious*, not curious — *not-incurious*, not not-curious; he makes a very modest claim for himself. Cf. also the preceding line.

l. 75, *snakestone*, any hard substance used as a remedy for snake-bites, whether applied externally or pounded up and taken internally. Samples of snakestone from Ceylon, examined by Prof. Michael Faraday (born 1791, died 1867), were found one of them to be of animal charcoal, one of chalk, one of some vegetable substance.[1]

l. 79, *were brought*, in his last letter before this.

P. 442, l. 3, *Vespasian*, born 9 A.D., made Roman Emperor 69, died 79; *his son*, Titus, who took Jerusalem and destroyed it 70 A.D.

l. 5, *balls*, eyeballs.

ll. 10–14, the description of the distance from Jerusalem to Bethany is not elegant, but it is very like a physician, probably quite like a physician of 1800 years ago.

l. 15, *travel-scrip*, travelling-bag: *scrip*, a small bag,

---

[1] See Berdoe, *Browning Cyclopædia*, ed. 1912, p. 160. Berdoe cites Tennant, *Ceylon*, 3d ed., I, 200.

wallet, satchel (cf. Matt. 10 : 10 and often in the Gospels, version of 1611).

l. 16, *Jewry*, place where Jews live, here the Jews' country, Judæa, — used with a touch of contempt.

l. 17, *viscid*, sticky; *choler*, bile.

l. 18, *tertians*, intermittent fevers occurring every other day, — called *tertian* (from Latin *tertianus*, of, or pertaining to, the third — *tertius*), because in the days when the name arose it was the custom to count both ends of a period of time. Cf. the N. T. writers' counting Fri. afternoon to Sun. morning as three days and using the phrase "on the third day" in referring to the resurrection of Christ. Cf. also "after eight days" (Jn. 20 : 26), meaning a week later.

l. 19, *falling-sickness*, epilepsy.

ll. 20 sqq., *there's a spider here etc.* The use of spiders to some extent in medical practice is ancient and had a long vogue. It is not nearly so revolting as many things in the therapeutics of bygone centuries. What Karshish was about to say was how to make a tincture, or else a decoction, of these spiders as a remedy for epilepsy, but it is too valuable a secret to risk. The particular spider referred to is probably the Zebra spider (*Epiblemum scenicum*). It belongs to the tribe of *Saltigradæ*, or leaping spiders (including especially those that lie in wait and leap on their prey). This tribe is of the *Wandering group*.[1] See Dr. H. McCook, in *Poet-Lore*, vol. I, p. 518.

l. 24, *runagate*, fugitive, vagabond; *this*, the letter he is writing.

ll. 25, 26, *His service*, in carrying the letter, is to pay me for treatment I've given him, viz. blowing a sublimate up

---

[1] Walcknaer divides spiders into five principal groups, distinguished by their habits.

his nose to help his ailing eye; a *sublimate* is any substance refined by melting, vaporizing, and then condensing, as is done *e.g.* with sulphur, iodine, camphor, or in the production of benzoic acid.

l. 30, *gum-tragacanth*, sold usually in dry flakes and employed for mucilage and similar uses in place of gum-arabic. It is procured from several species of shrubs of the genus *Astragalus*.

l. 32, *porphyry*, hard fine-grained rock, some varieties red, some purple, some green — usually with crystals of feldspar or quartz interspersed, — used, on account of its hardness, for such things as mortars.

l. 33, *in fine*, literally *in the end*, *i.e.* in conclusion, to sum it up.

l. 35, *Zoar*, a city near the south end of the Dead Sea.

l. 42, *tang*, a point, projection, sting; also, a flavor, taste.

l. 44, *the Man*, Lazarus, as presently comes out.

l. 53, *wit*, in the earlier and broader sense — mind, intellect, understanding.

l. 54, *subinduced*, literally *under-induced*, *i.e.* caused or started indirectly.

l. 57, *exhibition*, in the medical sense — " the act of administering as a remedy."

ll. 60 sqq. The idea that disease is due to possession by an evil spirit is ancient and widespread. Cf. the healing miracles in many instances in the New Testament.

l. 64, *conceit*, in the more general sense — concept, idea.

l. 71, *or . . . or*, either . . . or.

l. 76, *'Sayeth*, he sayeth. Cf. our use of *says* without a subject, in reporting a man's remarks.

l. 77, *diurnal*, daily — in the sense here of being daily met with.

l. 78, *figment*, something invented or imagined.

l. 82, *after-life*, the life which Karshish finds Lazarus living, after his experience of death and resurrection, or after this "figment" got fastened in his mind.

l. 84, *sanguine*, in the literal sense — full-blooded, (Latin *sanguis*, gen. *sanguinis*, blood).

l. 87, *as*, as if.

P. 443, l. 3, *premise*, present as introduction, explain beforehand.

l. 5, *inquisition*, keen searching inquiry.

ll. 28–50. The condemnation of Lazarus' point of view and actions is entirely from Karshish's point of view and comes from his testing those actions by his own scale of values. This he admits when he adds in l. 37 parenthetically "Far as I see." All the words "witless," "preposterously," "wrongly," are to be taken with the qualification — *as far as Karshish understands*.

l. 61, *a match* cannot, of course, be in our everyday sense or Browning has made an absurd slip. It must be taken in a more general sense of any means of starting a fire or setting off an explosion.

l. 62, *Greek fire*, the use of liquid fire is as ancient as Assyria (as is shown by representations on the monuments), *i.e.* such inflammable things as sulphur, tar, petroleum, nitre, were thrown on the enemy. The mixtures used later were no doubt more carefully made and more effective. Regular *Greek fire* is not known until the siege of Constantinople 673 A.D. Although something of the sort was undoubtedly known in the first century, the particular combination which became famous as Greek fire was not known then and Browning has made a mistake in having Karshish write the phrase.

l. 63, *He*, Lazarus.

l. 69, *that*, the spiritual life; *this*, the earthly life.

P. 444, l. 37, *leech*, physician.

l. 71, *blue-flowering borage*, the common borage (*Borago officinalis*), a plant which was for many centuries highly esteemed and supposed to possess qualities producing cordial and exhilarating effects; *Aleppo*, a city in north Syria, now capital of the Turkish vilayet of Aleppo.

l. 72, *nitrous*, containing nitre, *i.e.* potassium nitrate, saltpeter; *It is strange*, his thoughts slipping back to Lazarus.

l. 89, *ambiguous*, there's doubt as to what the Syrian may do with the letter — three things are mentioned, all of which are equally likely.

P. 445, l. 2, *so*, if God has become incarnate; *were*, subjunctive *would be*.

l. 3, *so*, same as in l. 2; *voice*, typographical error in this word in Globe Ed.

l. 5, *it*, a face like yours: the words of the line are really addressed to "Face, my hands fashioned," so we ought to say a face like yourself.

l. 6, *conceive*, misprinted in Globe Ed.

l. 9, *He*, the one who, Lazarus says, raised him from the dead.

II. Bishop Blougram's Apology, pp. 456–467

Browning gives us here a very interesting discussion. Much that is said, however, in the vein of defending superficial success and compromise with convictions and lack of out and out frankness with the public, is unlike Browning's genuine attitude. Browning himself has safeguarded this point by entering a caveat at the end:[1]

[1] The appendix (p. 467, ll. 30 sqq.) to the monologue is added on purpose to guard against our thinking that Browning supposed he had really justified a man in Bishop Blougram's attitude.   Notice chiefly ll. 39–64.

"Over his wine so smiled and talked his hour
    Sylvester Blougram, . . .
    With Gigadibs the literary man,
    Who played with spoons, explored his plate's design,
    And ranged the olive-stones about its edge."

5. Browning's sympathy with the Roman Catholic Church is one of the most interesting things in his nature. Extreme Protestant as he was, the mystic in him responded profoundly to much that he found in the Catholic Church, his æsthetic sense felt strongly the appeal of the artistic side of the Church's worship, and he honored the genuine piety which he knew in so many members of the Roman Communion. Protestant cavillers and controversialists should remember that Robert Browning, after many years in Italy in the midst of the Roman Catholic Church, makes the finest figure of nobility and self-sacrifice in his poems a young Roman Catholic priest, Giuseppe Caponsacchi in *The Ring and the Book*. It is not surprising, then, that in *Bishop Blougram's Apology* we find Browning stating the case of a doubting Roman Catholic Bishop and defending his view of life and his accepting the honors and emoluments of his office as well as a genuine ecclesiastic could do it, — and probably much in the same line in which a bishop of such mental make-up would have to speak, if he "made a clean breast of it" like this.

6. The figure that runs through the poem, often recurring, is of life as a voyage and our adapting our luggage to our cabin-space.

7. But the chief interest in *Bishop Blougram's Apology* is the discussion of Faith, and the principles laid down affect Protestantism as much as Catholicism — are, indeed, universal and apply inside or outside of any form and all forms of church organization. It is hard to begin

to quote without quoting great sections of the poem.
Some of the points in the argument are these:

a. Sheer unbelief is as hard to keep as sheer belief is.
Blougram proposes that we throw faith overboard: now
being sheer unbelievers what have we? We now have
unbelief disturbed by belief, just as we had belief shaken
by unbelief:[1]

> "All we have gained then by our unbelief
> Is a life of doubt diversified by faith,
> For one of faith diversified by doubt."

Half a page preceding these lines should be quoted in connection with them.

b. If you begin to believe, there's no drawing the line:[2]

> "some way must be, —
> Once feel about, and soon or late you hit
> Some sense in which it might be, after all.
> Why not 'The Way, the Truth, the Life?'"

c. On the other hand, if you begin to cut away things
which you count non-essential as matters of faith, begin to
clear off "excrescences," it is difficult to stop:[3]

> "First cut the Liquefaction,[4] what comes last
> But Fichte's clever cut at God himself?"

d. Faith is the positive attitude of mind without which
nothing is accomplished. Faith is constructive and
dynamic, and the great things done in the world have

---

[1] P. 458, ll. 59–61.   [2] P. 458, ll. 44–47.   [3] P. 464, ll. 60, 61.

[4] The Liquefaction of that portion of the blood of St. Januarius preserved
in a crystal phial in the cathedral of Naples. The miracle is alleged to take
place on special occasions, and regularly in public on St. Januarius' Day,
Sept. 19th. Cf. p. 464, ll. 43–47. See discussion of the miracle in art.
Januarius by Herbert Thurston, S. J., of London, in the *Catholic Encyclopedia*,
New York, 1910, vol. VIII, pp. 295–297. Browning here uses belief in it as
an illustration of crass credulity.

been due to faith — faith in *something*.   Browning gives
many illustrations : *e.g.* a man is crazy who thinks unbelief
can make a Napoleon : [1]

> "Be a Napoleon, and yet disbelieve —
> Why, the man's mad, friend, take his light away !"

Faith is the fire : [2]

> "fire and life
> Are all, dead matter's nothing, we agree :
> And be it a mad dream or God's very breath,
> The fact's the same, — belief's fire, once in us,
> Makes of all else mere stuff to show itself."

e. Morality is rooted in faith in some sort of invisible
things.   Morality cannot be accounted for solely as having
been an evolution from expediency.   And few who put
themselves down as sheer unbelievers are willing to live
consistently with that profession.[3]

f. Faith is a sound instinct : [4]

> "You own your instincts? why, what else do I,
> Who want, am made for, and must have a God
> Ere I can be aught, do aught?"

g. We are not altogether helpless in the matter of whether
we believe or not.   Will and desire have some part in it.
And Bishop Blougram considers that a man may choose to
such an extreme as to say : [5]

> "I absolutely and peremptorily
> Believe !"

h. But doubts will come.   And doubt is not wrong nor
inconsistent with faith :

> "If you desire faith — then you've faith enough." [6]

[1] P. 461, ll. 34, 35.   [2] P. 462, ll. 47–51.
[3] P. 465, ll. 44–70.   [4] P. 465, ll. 75–77.
[5] P. 459, ll. 7, 8.   [6] P. 463, l. 39.

Faith unmixed with doubt is impossible: [1]

> "Pure faith indeed — you know not what you ask!"

It could not be borne.

> "With me, faith means perpetual unbelief
> Kept quiet like the snake 'neath Michael's foot
> Who stands calm just because he feels it writhe." [2]

8. The poem has woven into it some of the threads of Browning's best philosophy:

a. The good service done by evil in the world: [3]

> "And that's what all the blessed evil's for."

b. The main thing — "to wake, not sleep:" [4]

> "I say, faith is my waking life:
> One sleeps, indeed, and dreams at intervals,
> We know, but waking's the main point with us,
> And my provision's for life's waking part.
> Accordingly, I use heart, head, and hand
> All day, I build, scheme, study, and make friends;
> And when night overtakes me, down I lie,
> Sleep, dream a little, and get done with it,
> The sooner the better, to begin afresh.
> What's midnight doubt before the dayspring's faith?"

c. The good of the struggle within a man, set forward in the grotesque and quite unforgettable picture of God pulling upward on the man and Satan pulling downward — and so he grows (we might almost say they stretch him by their pulling): [5]

> "No, when the fight begins within himself,
> A man's worth something.   God stoops o'er his head,
> Satan looks up between his feet — both tug —
> He's left, himself, i' the middle: the soul wakes
> And grows.   Prolong that battle through his life!
> Never leave [6] growing till the life to come!"

[1] P. 463, ll. 52 sqq.   [2] P. 463, ll. 71–73.   [3] P. 463, l. 59.
[4] P. 459, ll. 8–17; ll. 18–28 should also be quoted, they continue the same line of thought.   [5] P. 464, ll. 10–15.   [6] leave off.

9. If I may quote just one passage more, — this time to illustrate the picturesqueness with which Bishop Blougram carries forward his argument, let it be this one. After proposing that we divest ourselves of faith and see how we come out, he goes on : [1]

> "How can we guard our unbelief?
> Just when we are safest, there's a sunset-touch,
> A fancy from a flower-bell, some one's death,
> A chorus-ending from Euripides, —
> And that's enough for fifty hopes and fears
> As old and new at once as nature's self,
> To rap and knock and enter in our soul,
> Take hands and dance there, a fantastic ring,
> Round the ancient idol, on his base again, —
> The grand Perhaps!"

III. CLEON, pp. 467–471

We were speaking of Browning's ability to put himself in the place of one who had grown up in an entirely different civilization, and of *An Epistle* as an illustration of this. Another illustration of the same power is found in *Cleon*.

1. This also is a letter.

a. It is written by an imaginary poet (who is not only poet, but sculptor, painter, philosopher, and musician).[2] Browning, at the head of the poem, begins a quotation from St. Paul's address on the Areopagus in Athens (Acts 17 : 28) : "As certain also of your own poets have said, For we are also his offspring." The words given by Paul, "For we are also his offspring," [3] are from the *Phænomena* of Aratus,

---

[1] P. 458, ll. 30, 32–40. [2] P. 468, ll. 33–53.

[3] The words in a slightly different form are found in Cleanthes' *Hymn to Zeus* (4th century B.C.), where we read : "For thine offspring are we; therefore will I hymn thy praises and sing thy might forever." Paul's using the phrase "As certain also of your own poets have said" may easily

a Stoic poet of Soli [1] in Cilicia, in the third century B.C. It is not likely that Browning means to imply that he thought Paul quoted from an unknown poet for whom Browning invents the name Cleon. But Browning takes this phrase to introduce a letter purporting to be from a Greek poet, just as Paul uses the words to introduce his quotation from Aratus: *i.e.* Paul cites one poet, Browning cites another, who writes this letter.

b. This letter from the poet Cleon is to a king Protus "in his Tyranny." This is in the earlier Greek sense: [2] τύραννος (*turannos*), an absolute ruler of one of the Greek states, kind and good very likely, but king in an unlimited monarchy; thus we read of Pisistratus (born about 612 B.C., died 527 B.C.), "tyrant of Athens," a mild and beneficent ruler, and of the "tyrants" of other Greek cities; "his Tyranny," then, means his absolute sovereignty, or it may mean the territory ruled by such a king. Browning's poem does not indicate in what part of Greece his king Protus rules. [3]

c. This king is a patron of art and has sent Cleon rich gifts and a congratulatory letter, and has asked him certain questions. The nature of his congratulations and the nature of his questions we readily learn from the poet's answer.

imply that he knew the sentiment to have been expressed by more than one Greek poet. It is possible that the name Cleon for his poet was suggested to Browning by the name Cleanthes.

[1] Not a native of Paul's own city Tarsus, as is so often stated, but of Soli (or Pompeiopolis, as it was called after being rebuilt by Pompey the Great), a city on the coast southwest of Tarsus, in the same province of Cilicia in Asia Minor.

[2] The use of *tyrant*, however, meaning a ruler unjust and despotic, arose already in the later days of the ancient Greek civilization.

[3] The reference to the phare (p. 468, l. 41) proves nothing, because it is only a general word for lighthouse. The reference to the Pœcile of Athens proves nothing except that Protus had never seen it (see ll. 43, 44).

d. The king's letter has just been handed to Cleon, and he is writing his reply as the master of the king's galley unloads the gifts.[1]

e. The time is in the first Christian century, during the missionary preaching of Paul, the Apostle of Jesus Christ. This is evident from the close of the letter[2] which shows that the king has asked Cleon about Paul and that Cleon knows Paul has preached somewhere in the vicinity of his island. Paul was undoubtedly martyred near the close of the reign of Nero Cæsar, who committed suicide June 9th, in the year 68. Paul's death was some time 64 to 67 A.D. This letter belongs to a time at least ten years earlier, *i.e.* when Paul was in Greece and neighboring parts of the Empire, in the years 50–55 A.D.[3]

f. Cleon is a pagan Greek, with all the learning, sense of art, and contempt for the Jews[4] which a cultured Greek would have.

g. He is writing "from the sprinkled isles" of Greece,[5] "that o'erlace the sea" like lilies, — probably the Cyclades, a group in the Ægean Sea, east of the southern end of Greece.

2. The only words that need explanation are:

P. 468, l. 37, *epos* (Gk. ἔπος), an epic poem.

l. 41, *the phare*, lighthouse. The word is derived from

---

[1] P. 467, ll. 78–83. Notice the description (p. 468, ll. 1–8) of how one of the slaves brings to Cleon wine in a cup which the king himself has used.

[2] P. 471, ll. 55–71. Paul himself has not preached on that island, but has been near enough so that some of his converts have preached there.

[3] In having Cleon at this period address a letter "to Protus in his Tyranny," Browning forgets the historical situation. As a matter of fact there were no sovereigns in any part of Greece in the first century A.D., but the whole country was a province of the Roman Empire, — the province of Achaia.

[4] P. 471, ll. 61–67. Paul is to him "a mere barbarian Jew."

[5] P. 467, ll. 74–76.

Pharos, the name of a rocky island off the city of Alexandria, Egypt. Alexander the Great, who founded the city 332 B.C., connected the island with the mainland by a mole [1] (called the *Heptastadium*, because it was seven stadia long — about four-fifths of a mile), thus providing two harbors. Along this mole a street was later constructed, making Pharos a suburb of Alexandria. On the northeast point of the island the famous lighthouse stood for 1600 years. It was built chiefly by Ptolemy I (died 283 B.C., founder of the Greek dynasty in Egypt) and completed by his son Ptolemy Philadelphus (Ptolemy II, born 309, died 247 B.C.). It was hardly a lighthouse in our modern sense, but a great beacon-tower, with a fire kept constantly burning on it. The Greek word *pharos* (φάρος), then, came to be used for any such tower.

l. 43, *Pœcile* (also in English *Stoa Pœcile*, and *Poicile; Gk. ποικίλη, many-colored*, or in full ἡ στοὰ ποικίλη, or ἡ ποικίλη στοά, *the many-colored portico*), the famous "porch," or covered colonnade, in Athens, where Zeno, founder of the Stoics, taught and from which the Stoics derived their name. It was decorated with paintings,[2] one of the artists being Polygnotus of Thasos (5th century B.C.). It cannot be that Browning is ignorant of Polygnotus' work in the Pœcile and accredits the whole to Cleon. He probably means that there were paintings there by artists whose names we do not know, among whom he places his Cleon. But the language (ll. 43, 44) "The Pœcile . . . is mine too" sounds as if Cleon claimed all the paintings there as his work.

---

[1] This mole still remains and has been increased by alluvial deposits until it is a broad neck of land.

[2] P. 468, ll. 43, 44: "o'er-storied its whole length . . . with painting," *i.e.* covered its whole length with stories told in pictures.

1. 50, *combined the moods*. The various sequences of tones and semitones in the diatonic scale — the variety depending upon where you begin — are called *moods*, or *modes* (usually *modes*). Thus, *e.g.*, on a piano key-board, taking the key of C (*i.e.* omitting the black keys), if we begin with D, the octave D to D gives the *Dorian mode*, E to E the *Phrygian*, F to F the *Lydian*, G to G the *Mixolydian*. The *modes* furnish great variety in the relative position of the tones and semitones, and a corresponding variety in the effect of the music, some being bright, some sombre, and therefore different modes being suitable for different subjects and occasions. The Greek music was the basis on which the music of the Christian Church was developed, and the principles of Greek music have persisted in the music of the Church. In the earlier history of Church music, four modes were recognized, called *authentic modes*, and these are thought to have been adopted directly from Greek music. Later, four *plagal modes* were added, and still later others have been added and some made by combining some already accepted. The development of Church music was gradual and never the work of one man nor of a few, but the chief stages in it are associated with the names of Ambrose (born about 340, died 397), Bishop of Milan, and Pope Gregory the Great (born 542, made Pope 590, died 604). The Gregorian music is still extensively used — is, indeed, now officially the music of the Latin Church. The modes in it are usually designated by numbers, as *e.g.* the *first mode*, the *second mode*, the *sixth mode*. In modern music only two modes are recognized, the Major and the Minor.[1]

[1] These, although spoken of as the Major and Minor *key* and Major and Minor *scales*, and although they may involve sharps and flats, are essentially *modes*.

P. 471, l. 58, *Paulus*, Paul.

l. 59, *Christus*, Christ.

ll. 59, 69.   This echo of rumors in regard to Paul, confusing him with Christ, gives, no doubt, a faithful rep-
resentation of the confusion in the minds of most of
the people of Achaia and other provinces, — knowing
only vaguely and indifferently of the new doctrine and its
chief promulgator.

3. The poem is very gracefully written. It is not
necessary to choose illustrations out of its almost uniform
excellence, but perhaps these lines are the best:

P. 467, l. 83, "Royal with sunset, like a thought of thee."
P. 468, l. 32, "Within the eventual element of calm."
P. 471, l. 49, "Freed by the throbbing impulse we call death."

4. The main points in the poem, in answer to the king's
congratulations and questions:

a. P. 468, ll. 33 sqq.   The king has congratulated Cleon
on how much he has accomplished.   Cleon's answer is: It
is even so.   He has done all these things.   Cleon's mind
represents the growth of culture.   He is superior to the
ancients, his mind is more composite and therefore greater
than the simpler minds of the past.   They were each great
in one line and in his own line each of the great in the past
may have easily exceeded Cleon.   But he is capable of
appreciating the best each one of them has done.   At the
same time he has wider interests and more varied activity.

b. P. 469, ll. 53 sqq.   Has not Cleon therefore attained
the crown and proper end of life?   How does he face
death?   Having gained so much and having given so much
to enrich the life of the world, can it not be said of him
that he does not die?   No, says Cleon.   He sees that
relentless progress is a law in all around him.   But the

individual is lost. The progress is accomplished by the individual's adding himself, his life and work, to the world's life and losing himself. But to say that this is immortality is juggling with words. There is small comfort for the individual in the progress of the race, if the individual soul perishes. The individual has not really achieved immortality. To survive incorporate with the life of humanity, even to live as an individual in the memory of men, is not really to be alive, — and Cleon shrinks from it, he loves life so much.

c. P. 470, ll. 77 sqq. But, insists the king in his letter, such a poet or artist lives in his works. Cleon repeats that this is not life. The king has tripped upon a word. Knowing how and showing how to live are very different from actually living. Knowing what joy is is different from feeling joy. Writing of love is not the same as loving and being loved. If Sappho and Æschylus live still, as the king says they do, let them come and do what a living man can do. No, no, the idea which the king has so generously expressed,[1] that he cannot face death as cheerfully as Cleon can because he leaves no works in which to live as Cleon does — this is exactly contrary to the case. Cleon's "fate is deadlier still." For Cleon, after all his intensity of life out of which these works were made, himself will be dead, while his works will be alive to mock him.[2] Cleon says he has thought of the possibility of personal immortality, a future state with joy enough to satisfy the "joy-hunger" which we have here. Then

[1] See quotation from his letter, p. 469, ll. 63–75. Cf. p. 471, l. 26.

[2] The mockery consists in this situation: that the works will still have their part in the life of men, while the personality which gave them being will be extinct. This passage (p. 471, ll. 27–41) is the most poignant in the poem. Surely it is out of Browning's own love of life and his recoil from being blotted out.

death would be only emancipation. But he judges it is not a fact, or else Zeus would have revealed it to us.

d. P. 471, ll. 54 sqq. Farewell and postscript. The postscript refers to the king's question as to Paul and his preaching. It gives the cultured Greek's attitude. The king's servant has a letter for Paulus, if he can find him,— doubtless to ask the same old questions mankind has always been asking.

IV. ONE WORD MORE, pp. 472-474

This was the epilogue to *Men and Women*. Those two volumes contained, as published, 50 other poems[1] and this epilogue — hence usually spoken of as 51 poems. *One Word More* is really a dedication of the two volumes to Mrs. Browning. At its head stands *To E. B. B.* (Elizabeth Barrett Browning) *1855*. It is signed *R. B.* at the end.

1. *The Metre.*

a. One Word More is written in *trochaic pentameter, i.e.* five-foot lines, the normal foot being of two syllables with the accent on the first syllable. Thus *e.g.* the first line is regular :

Thére they | áre, my | fíf-ty | mén and | wóm-en.

b. The usual English blank verse, or "heroic" verse, is *iambic* pentameter, *i.e.* each line of five feet, the normal foot being of two syllables, accented on the second syllable. Thus *e.g.* a regular line from *Cleon* :[2]

They gíve | thy lét | ter tó | me é | ven nów.

(1) The five-foot iambic blank verse is that in which the greatest poetry in the English language is written, — the

[1] The larger part of them now distributed in the collected works under other headings, as we have already pointed out. See Browning's note, p. 472, bottom of 1st column.

[2] P. 467, l. 78.

major works of Shakespeare, Milton, Tennyson, Browning, and many others. (2) But the regular line, with five feet and every other syllable stressed, would become intolerably mechanical and monotonous. Hence there have arisen, for the sake of melody and flexibility, a great variety of substitutions [1] in the line.

c. Similarly, in handling five-foot trochaic, Browning practices some substitution, but not with anywhere near the freedom which he and other masters use in handling five-foot iambic.

d. One Word More is the largest piece of five-foot trochaic in the English language. Lines of five-foot trochaic are found: *e.g.* in Tennyson's *Vision of Sin* and his *Ode on the Death of the Duke of Wellington.* But this of Browning's is the only piece of any considerable length in this metre in English. Perhaps p. 473, l. 76, may refer to the uniqueness of the metre: [2]

"Lines I write the first time and the last time."

e. It appears that in Bohemian poetry, the usual five-foot line is trochaic, just as in English the usual is iambic. At least that is what I understand Omond to mean when he says: [3]

"In Bohemian literature, I understand, *falling* rhythm is as natural as *rising* with us; the metre of *One Word More* is normal, that of *Paradise Lost* exotic."

[1] This matter of the substitution of other feet for the iambic, along with the other technicalities of this verse, is too long to discuss here. The reader is referred to any standard works on English Metre, but especially to Mayor's *Chapters on English Metre* (2d ed. 1901), where there is a careful inquiry into the usage of the best masters.

[2] The whole passage (section XIII), however, probably refers to the nature and general style of the poem.

[3] T. S. Omond, *A Study of Metre*, London, 1903, p. 64. Omond throughout discards the usual terminology, and calls feet "periods" — those accented on the first part "falling rhythm," accented on the latter part "rising rhythm."

2. *Notes.*

a. Two of the footnotes in the Globe Edition need a little modification. Both refer to Rafael's sonnets :

P. 472, l. 33, "Rafael made a century of sonnets."

Note 2, "There is no reason to believe this to be the fact."

P. 472, l. 54, "You and I will never read that volume."

Note 8, "Really a book of drawings, not sonnets."

The Editor's assertions are too sweeping :

(1) It is supposed that the book of Rafael's kept by Guido Reni and lost after his death contained drawings.

(2) But it is known that Rafael wrote some three or four love-sonnets on the back of sketches, and these are still preserved. One of them is in the British Museum.

(3) It may be that similarly the 100 drawings in the book lost had each one a sonnet on the back, — that Browning had some information that this was the case, or guessed that it might be so.

b. The following notes in addition to, or in completion of, those in the Globe Edition :

P. 472, l. 33, *Rafael* (in English more often *Raphael*), famous painter, born 1483, died 1520 ; *century*, 100, — now narrowed down to a measure of time but formerly used for 100 of anything.[1]

l. 37, *these*, the Madonnas ; *but one*, supply *might view*.

l. 38, *Who that one ?* Browning refers to the story popularly told of Rafael's attachment for a baker's daughter in Rome. The story rests on slight foundations, if any. Her name is given as Margherita, and the painting of which she is supposed to be the original is in the Barberini Palace

---

[1] Thus a Roman legion was divided into centuries of soldiers, Shakespeare (*Cymbeline*, IV. ii. 391) has "a century of prayers," and we still say "a century-run" made *e.g.* on a bicycle.

in Rome. It is signed by Rafael on a bracelet worn by the figure. Since about 1750, the picture has been called *La Fornarina* (*i.e.* "The Bakeress"). The portrait also named *La Fornarina*, in the Uffizi Gallery in Florence, is not by Rafael but by Sebastian del Piombo (1485–1547), and does not resemble the face in Rafael's painting in the Barberini Palace. The same should be said of another *La Fornarina* by the same Sebastian in the Old Museum, Berlin.

l. 50, *San Sisto*, Saint Sixtus the Martyr (Sixtus II, elected Bishop of Rome Aug. 31st, 257, beheaded Aug. 6th, 258, in the persecution under the Emperor Valerian); he *names* a Madonna, *i.e.* it is named from him the *Madonna di San Sisto*, the *Sistine Madonna*, because it was painted as an altarpiece for the Church of San Sisto at Piacenza and has in it a figure representing St. Sixtus in an attitude of adoration (at the left as you face the picture), — it is now in the Royal Gallery in Dresden; *Foligno*, a town in Central Italy, — the *Madonna of Foligno* is now in the Vatican.

l. 51. The picture referred to is in the Pitti Palace at Florence and represents the Madonna appearing to a votary in a vision. It is called the *Madonna del Granduca*.

l. 52. The picture called *La Belle Jardinière*, in the Louvre in Paris, shows the Madonna seated in a garden among lilies.

l. 55, *Guido Reni*, eminent Italian painter, born 1575, died 1642.

l. 60, *Dante* (born 1265, died 1321) gives an account of this incident in the *Vita Nuova*, xxxv.

l. 61, *Beatrice*, Beatrice Portinari, who was idealized by Dante until she became the centre of his poetic inspiration.

P. 473, l. 13, *Bice*, contraction for Beatrice, used affectionately as a diminutive or nickname.

l. 29, *Heaven's gift* etc. — earth mars Heaven's gift, takes something away from it.

ll. 30 sqq. refer to Moses' smiting the rock for water (Ex. 17 : 1–7, Num. 20 : 1–11), and the implied comparison is to an artist's serving an ungrateful world.

l. 51, *Egypt's flesh-pots*, in the murmuring of the Hebrews against Moses (Ex. 16 : 2, 3).

l. 53, *Sinai-forehead's cloven brilliance*, when Moses received the Law, may refer to the lightning on the forehead of the mountain (Ex. 19 : 9, 16, 18) or to the shining of Moses' face when he came down (Ex. 34 : 29, 30).

l. 57, *Jethro's daughter*, Moses' wife Zipporah (Ex. 2 : 16, 21, cf. 3 : 1).

l. 58, *The Æthiopian bondslave*, another wife of Moses (Num. 12 : 1), not so well known as Zipporah.

P. 474, l. 4, *missal-marge*, margin on the page of a missal, *i.e.* a book containing the Mass for regular and for special occasions.

ll. 23–35. They saw the new moon in Florence, saw it grow into a full moon; then they came to London, and see it now in the last quarter there.

l. 27, *Fiesole*, a town on a hill near Florence, readily seen from the city. This is why the new moon came

"Drifted [1] over Fiesole by twilight."

l. 29, *Samminiato*, San Miniato, a famous church in Florence. Cf. *Giovambattista*,[2] *i.e.* Giovanni Battista (John Baptist).

ll. 36 sqq. This myth in many forms is woven into Literature. Cf. Keats' *Endymion*.

---

[1] Passive participle modifying *she* (l. 28), — in the same construction as the active participle *curving* (l. 26).

[2] *The Ring and the Book*, p. 664, l. 13.

l. 39, *mythos* (Gk. μῦθος), a speech, a story (at first a true story) ; then a myth.

l. 42, *Zoroaster*, founder of the ancient Persian religion, which is spoken of as Zoroastrianism; it survives (in a modified form, no doubt) as the religion of the Parsees in India. It is impossible to get any definite information as to when he lived. It was probably 1000 years B.C. or more.

l. 43, *Galileo*, an Italian astronomer, born 1564, died 1642.

l. 44, *Dumb to Homer*, cf. the Hymn to Diana in the *Iliad*, XXI ; *dumb to Keats*, cf. his *Endymion*. The point is that the moon in love with a mortal might turn and show him what *not even* those most interested in the moon — Zoroaster, Galileo, Homer, Keats — have ever seen.

ll. 45 sqq., speculation as to what the other side of the moon might be like, if she turned round for a mortal whom she loved. Beginning with l. 63, the poem goes on to make two applications of this figure : (1) ll. 63–66, Browning or any man has "two soul-sides" one of which is shown only to a woman whom he loves; (2) ll. 66–76, Browning does see the other side of Mrs. Browning's personality, — he stands with the world and praises that side which all see, but also he passes around to the other side and sees her soul as the world never sees it.

ll. 51 sqq., at Mt. Sinai (Ex. 24 : 1–11, especially vss. 9–11).

l. 56, *the bodied heaven*, a phrase adapted from Ex. 24 : 10, "as it were the body of heaven in his clearness." "The body of heaven" was the sky, which in ancient days was supposed to be a substantial thing — "the firmament."

ll. 77–80, an illustration of what in Rhetoric is technically called *Chiasmus* (Gk. χιασμός, a placing crosswise, — derived ultimately from the letter χ). If we yoke up the lines as they grammatically go, we shall see the crossing, *i.e.* one statement is ll. 77 and 79, the other is ll. 78 and 80 — thus:

> "Oh, their Rafael of the dear Madonnas,
> Oh, their Dante of the dread Inferno,
> Wrote one song — and in my brain I sing it,
> Drew one angel — borne, see, on my bosom!"

3. *The argument in the poem.*

Section I. Browning dedicates the 50 poems in *Men and Women* to Mrs. Browning — she has his heart already — let her have his brain also, *i.e.* let her have these poems, the product of his brain.

Sections II–VII. Cases of men who have done, or undertaken to do, something out of their usual line for one they love most, — something they wouldn't try to do for the public.

Section VIII. Statement of what is the point in the preceding illustrations.

Sections IX–XI. Discussion of the reason why a man wishes to do as in the cases cited, — the reason being that the public mars the fineness of a man's doing and he has to sustain toward them a fixed attitude and does not really make his best known. Consequently, when he does want to express his best to one whom he loves, he feels like adopting a different vehicle from that used in dealing with the world. Further illustrations, these being from Moses' experience with the Hebrew people.

Sections XII–XIV. Application of the foregoing, *i.e.* of the instincts and principles discussed, to Browning's attitude toward Mrs. Browning. He is unable to turn to another form of art for her sake to express his love, — he can only write verse. But with wealth of illustrations he shows that a man with only one artistic ability may use it in a way to him unique, for a particular purpose. So Browning writes now, as never before and never again, — the poem being this *One Word More*.

Sections xv–xviii. A figure from the moon and what a man might see if she really loved him, as in the classical myth. So with a personality, only love really knows it. Mrs. Browning knows Browning[1] because of their love, and for the same reason he knows her.[2] Each sees in the other's nature what is never shown to the world.

Section xix. Mrs. Browning fulfills for Browning the desire which made Rafael turn from painting to write sonnets and made Dante turn from poetry to draw an angel.

4. *The charm of the poem* is elusive, but none the less real, and is, indeed, rather haunting. We come back to *One Word More* scores of times, and it is always new and exquisite. The charm may be due partly to the unusual metre, partly to the fact that the poem is a mosaic of allusions to Art and Literature, so that it "holds out" well no matter how much we read it, partly to the subtle truth presented in it.[3] The passion and devotion which actuate it also help in its hold on us.

[1] P. 474, ll. 23, "Not but that you know me!" and 66, "This I say of me," and the general statement ll. 63–65.

[2] The application to Mrs. Browning (ll. 66–76) is naturally longer and finer, — how on the side of her personality away from the world he enters the

"Silent silver lights and darks undreamed of."

[3] Browning had the ability to discuss, or at least to state, very subtle facts of human nature. For another example in a short poem, see *Two in the Campagna* (pp. 250, 251).

VIII

SAUL AND IN A BALCONY

I. Saul, pp. 239–245

Published as follows: The first nine sections in *Dramatic Romances and Lyrics*, 1845; the whole poem as now in vol. II of *Men and Women*, 1855. Although ten years elapsed between the appearance of the first part and that of the remainder of the poem, the reader does not detect it in passing from section IX into the following sections. The discussion of *Saul* is put at this point in the course because more than half of the poem belongs to *Men and Women*, and because, though one of the most widely read of Browning's poems, it is also one of the most difficult.

1. *The Suggestion on which the Poem is Founded.*

This is found in 1 Sam. 16: 14–23. It is the account of Saul's illness and David's playing the harp before him. The passage should be carefully read before reading the poem.

2. *The Purpose of the Poem.*

a. Men sometimes wonder whether anything is worth while. They lose interest in life. It all seems "weary, stale, flat and unprofitable." Some of you may have passed through this experience. Many of you will have to. Why live? Why struggle? What does it all amount to? "Surely every man walketh in a vain show." Everything is dust and ashes, and life is just a wretched "mess," a game "not worth the candle."

b. Browning takes Saul as a type of those seized with such despair. Or perhaps Saul's case is too extreme to be typical. Saul's illness is described in the early history of the Hebrews, according to the time, as due to seizure by an evil spirit. Browning interprets it as a *lethargy,* — a loss of all interest in life, which condition paralyzes all effort of mind and body. Why make any effort? Nothing is of worth. Men who think there is something of worth in life are deceived. Let it all go.

c. What can stimulate a man like that to take an interest in life again? What *really makes life worth while?*

d. David, in the songs given him by Browning, answers the question. (1) It is the following day[1] when David relates how he went to Saul and what he said as he sang. (2) David, as he tells it, is back with his sheep, in the narrow valley of the Kidron, a brook near Jerusalem; he looks out toward the south to the city of Hebron, on the mountain in the distance.[2] (3) David tells how he came at the summons, was met by Abner, commander of Saul's army (1 Sam. 26:5), how he kissed Abner (the oriental fashion), then of his experience when, after praying, he entered Saul's tent.

3. *Some Details which David Gives Incidentally.*

Such details are vivid and interesting.

a. As to Saul himself: (1) his huge figure[3] (see 1 Sam. 9:1, 2, and 10:23) and his movements when stirred by the singing;[4] (2) his position among the people. We need

[1] P. 243, ll. 7–13. The whole of section XIV, after the first half line, is parenthetical and refers to the situation in which he finds himself the following morning. Cf. also p. 245, section XIX, especially ll. 12 sqq.

[2] P. 243, ll. 9, 11, 12.

[3] P. 240, ll. 4–6; cf. l. 42 and p. 243, ll. 30, 31.

[4] P. 240, ll. 42 sqq.; p. 241, ll. 40 sqq.; p. 243, ll. 13 sqq. Notice especially p. 243, ll. 33–40.

to revise our usual notion of the circumstances. We must not be misled by what we associate with the word "king." Browning's picture is more true to history. The Hebrews had gotten a foothold in the country and were struggling to maintain it. Saul, chosen as their first king, was practically a fighting chief. Hence David finds him, not in a palace, but in his camp.

b. The tent (described somewhat in section III) is of skins[1] or else of goats' hair.[2] In either case it is dark inside; hence David, coming from the sunlight outside, is unable to make out things until his eyes become accustomed to the gloom — he makes out the main tent-prop and the figure of Saul before the sunbeam gets in through the roof and shows him Saul clearly.[3]

c. The harpstrings in the days of David were of catgut or even of vegetable fibre. The intense heat would cause them to shrink, and so they might "snap 'neath the stress of the noontide." Hence the lilies (in section v, cf. section II), twined round the strings to keep them moist. The observation that there was no danger that heat would cause the strings to snap would hold true only if metal strings were used, and metal strings are later. Some types of harp are still equipped wholly or in part with gut strings.

d. Many details of customs you will notice in the songs: *e.g.* in section VII, marriage, funeral, and liturgical customs; in section VIII (ll. 42–44) and section XV (ll. 16–27), the dress of the chief; in section IX (p. 240, ll. 49 sqq.), hunting

---

[1] Tents at a very early period were probably of skins. Traces of such use of skins are found in the Old Testament, *e.g.* Ex. 26 : 14.

[2] Early in the history of the Hebrews, goats' hair was spun and woven by the women for such uses. See Ex. 35 : 26, also 36 : 14. Such tents were dark-colored, cf. Song of Solomon 1 : 5.

[3] P. 240, ll. 2–6.

SAUL

171

and food; again in section IX (p. 241, ll. 7–11), the office for the dying; in section XIII (ll. 43 sqq.), methods of commemorating the deeds of the great.

4. *Plan of Versification.*

a. The verse is rhymed *five-foot anapestic, i.e.* the normal line is made up of five periods, each composed of three syllables with the accent on the last syllable: thus *e.g.*

That exténds | to the séc | ond enclós | ure, I gróped | my way ón,[1]

or

The submís | sion of mán's | nothing - pér | fect to Gód's | all-compléte.[2]

But the verse is used with great freedom, as anapestic verse is by all skillful poets,[3] and the completely regular lines are not much more than half the whole number. The variations, as Browning handles the verse, consist chiefly in dropping one of the unaccented syllables at the beginning of a line, or in any other foot, except the last.[4]

b. Browning has worked out a device for emphasizing certain words. The plan is effective. The words strike the reader, whether he stops to analyze how it is done or not. This will be noticed at the end of section III:

"Then a sunbeam, that burst thro' the tent-roof, showed Saul."

At the end of section VI:

"But I stopped here: for here in the darkness Saul groaned."

And at the end of section IX:

---

[1] P. 239, l. 66. [2] P. 244, l. 3.

[3] See Joseph B. Mayor, *Handbook of Modern English Metre*, Cambridge, 1903, Chapter V.

[4] Sometimes there is an additional unaccented syllable after the close of the last foot, as *e.g.* p. 243, ll. 3, 4. In at least one case, Browning has four syllables in a foot, — p. 241, l. 6, last foot.

"Brought to blaze on the head of one creature — King Saul!"

There actually are in each of these lines only four feet,
and the *time* of two feet is given to the last foot.　Hence
the emphasis on "showed Saul," "Saul groaned," and
"King Saul," — *i.e.* the mind and voice involuntarily
slow up and give to the words the additional beat which
the rhythm requires.[1]

5. *The Steps by which David brings Saul back to an Interest in Life.*

David shows him, in an ascending scale, what is worth
living for.

a. David plays first the tunes that appeal to brutes
(sections v and vi).　The animals below man are many
of them very susceptible to music.　David is beginning
at the foundation — not argument nor the content of song,
but sheer sound — that is what attracts the lower animals.

Will this soothe and stimulate Saul?　No.　These tunes
which stir the lower animals provoke no sign from Saul.

b. Then David sings the everyday interests of human
life.　This is his second move (sections vii and viii).
These are the things that occupy the attention of most
people.　Life's hours are largely taken up with this round
of things — our conversation is chiefly about them.　The
points sung about are the things of importance in the
average life.　Each point is typical: The reapers' song
(typical of the social gathering), the lament for the dead,
the marriage chant, the organization of government[2] (or

[1] Such devices are common in poetry, and are used instinctively by good
artists.　The omission of one of the syllables of a foot, allowing the time to
fill up the space, is of a similar sort.

[2] Or do the lines (p. 240 ll. 36–38) refer to the building of a material
structure, as *e.g.* in connection with the walls of a city?　The uncertainty
arises from our inability to determine whether Browning meant us to take

of social institutions in general), the Levites' chorus as they go up to the altar (typical of the place which worship occupies in life). The order is curious: we would think the lament for the dead would be last. But the person described in these different songs is not the same man. The *observer*, whose life touches all these things described in the songs, continues the same man — you or I. And all these things are mingled just so in our living, *i.e.* we come in contact with joy and sorrow close together, — we are interested in feast, funeral, wedding, politics, religion — and these often in incongruous closeness to each other. Such are the things in which people in general are interested — the things that stimulate our thinking and our conversation.

Will these songs stir Saul? These songs, rehearsing the usual events of interest in life, call out from Saul only a groan and a movement of the head.

c. How can David stimulate Saul further, now that he has attracted his attention? David's third move is two-fold:

(1) He sings of the sheer joy of living (section IX, from the beginning to p. 241, l. 4). If we are well and normal, just being alive, tingling with life, ought to be its own reward. The joy of life is set forth as it would appeal to a red-blooded man of Saul's time.

(2) David points to the greatness of Saul's life in particular (the rest of section IX), — how much centres in him, how great is his opportunity — therefore how great his incentive to live the fullest life.

"buttress an arch" (l. 37) literally or figuratively. I used to think that it referred to the marriage, "our friends" (l. 38) being the pair just married. But the punctuation forbids that and shows that this is another independent song of the series. The fact that the "arch" is something to protect the friends of those who build it leads me to think that the arch is a system of government, the builders statesmen; or else that it stands for civilization and society, in which we all are builders.

This strikes into Saul, especially the shouting of his own name at the end, and he releases himself, letting go the cross-support on the tent-pole to which he had clung (section x). His movement is like the sliding of snow from a mountain in the warmth of spring.[1]

d. David is at a loss now what to sing next to stimulate Saul to live and do his work in the world (sections XI and XII). But presently thoughts develop which came to him when he was with his sheep, and he sings now (section XIII), saying that the real greatness of Saul is not in living a mere mortal life, but in his great deeds which will live after him — be recorded on the rock's face and on cedar tablets and in papyrus rolls, and hand his name and fame to posterity. This is one of the strongest desires of men, that their work shall not perish with them. Surely this will rouse Saul to see that life is good and to be eager to live it. Such is the fourth step.

This appeal restores Saul (section xv) to "his old motions and habitudes kingly." He is coming back to a realization that it is worth while to live, to achieve, to rule.

e. What shall David sing next to bring Saul completely into fullness of life? He drops the harp with which he had sung up to this time, and breaks out into exhortation (section XVI, "No harp more — no song more! outbroke —"), the fifth step. The rush of truth as to what makes life most worth living comes with some confusion in sections XVII and XVIII, consistently with David's enthusiasm as it is borne in upon him. If set forth in too orderly a way, it would not reflect the surging tide in David's

[1] P. 241, ll. 29–40, an elaborate description of the sliding of the snow from the mountain. This interrupts the account of what Saul did, — the account which begins near the middle of l. 27 and is continued near the middle of l. 40. Lines 29–40 unfortunately distract attention from Saul's movements, instead of making clearer what he did.

thoughts. It deals with things of supreme value, it is truth of the highest life in man. It is grounded in the infinite love of God, which must be a fact or else we exceed God, for we love. We find that God is infinitely beyond us in everything else. It must be, then, that there is an infinitude of love to match the infinitude of the rest of His nature. And this infinite love of God must issue in three things, and these are essential if man is to come to the fulfillment of the spiritual life:

(1) The immortality of man, not merely in his works, but the immortality of his living self.

(2) A way of redemption whereby God suffers for man, even as we are willing to suffer for those we love.

(3) A "human life of God" in the Messiah, the Christ, so that God may have perfect sympathy with the human struggle: this is the only way man can be saved.

Each of these strands is woven in more or less several times, but after all there is progress in the song. The fact that God infinitely surpasses us in every way, as far as we can see in His universe, is laid down first.[1] Then the necessity of believing that God is not inferior to us in the one element Love is strongly set forth.[2] The love of God issuing in some redemptive plan comes next,[3] such redemption involving the immortality of man.[4] The love of God compelling Him to suffer for man, else He is inferior to us who suffer for one another, is then taken up.[5] That this makes necessary the coming of the Divine into a human experience, or the union of Divine and human in one ex-

[1] P. 243, l. 46–p. 244, l. 4. Notice especially p. 243, ll. 51–58.
[2] P. 244, ll. 5–20, especially ll. 10–20.
[3] P. 244, ll. 21–36, especially ll. 27–33.
[4] P. 244, ll. 28, 34–36.
[5] P. 244, ll. 37–54, especially ll. 49–53.

perience, is the last point brought forward.[1] The immortality of man appears also in these closing lines of the song.

Such words as these in sections XVII and XVIII, put in the mouth of David, while more definite and theological than the Old Testament Messianic prophecy (especially of so early a time as 1000 B.C.), are not inconsistent with the longing of the Hebrews and their Messianic hope, at least as it developed in later centuries of their history.

6. *The Conclusion.*

Section XIX tells how the realization of the great things of the spiritual life, which had come upon David in his last song, made him aware of the living world of the unseen as he went home, and how even next morning he saw a new meaning in all Nature. The point in this section is that, when a man recognizes the presence of the redemptive power in the world, he sees the world as he never saw it before.

II. In a Balcony, pp. 475–486

Published in vol. II of *Men and Women*, 1855.

1. *The Nature of the Poem.*

It is simply conversation. There is only a little action. The dramatic motives are strong, but the piece is in no sense a drama, and was never called a drama by Browning. The piece is made up of one scene. A few directions are put in to make plain the going in and coming out.

2. *The Place.*

The conversation takes place in a balcony overlooking the street.[2]

a. You have often seen on a house such a balcony, projecting over the street or lawn (perhaps on top of the

[1] P. 244, ll. 55–62, especially ll. 57–62.   [2] P. 477, ll. 7–9.

porch), and entered by doors from the second floor, — a place to sit in summer. Many apartment houses have such a balcony connected with each suite of rooms.

b. This particular balcony, as we see from the poem, opens from the parlors and banquet-room of the Palace. To have the parlors on what we call the second floor (what they call there the first floor) is quite common on the Continent. So also very often in England, in attending some social function, you leave your wraps down stairs and are received in a drawing-room up stairs.

c. Those on this balcony are only six steps from where the others are.[1] They hear the music[2] even when the doors are closed, but it is especially noticeable when one goes in or out.[3] On this balcony the moon shines.[4] There are several pieces of statuary here,[5] also palms and magnolias.[6]

3. *The Persons.*

The persons involved in the conversation are:

a. The Queen. We gather readily from the conversation these facts: She is fifty years old,[7] thin[8] and already gray,[9] sole ruler of a considerable country (ruler with even despotic power[10]). She married unhappily years ago and is separated from her husband but not divorced.[11] With

---

[1] P. 475, l. 46; p. 476, l. 44.   [2] P. 478, l. 40; p. 486, l. 41.

[3] P. 479, stage direction following l. 23; p. 482, stage direction following l. 57.

[4] P. 481, l. 78; p. 482, l. 57. Cf. p. 478, l. 23.

[5] P. 478, ll. 31–34; p. 482, ll. 54–56.

[6] P. 479, ll. 40–42; p. 485, ll. 45–47. The palm and the magnolia mentioned can hardly be on a lawn or in a garden below, because this balcony is over a street (p. 477, ll. 7–9).

[7] P. 476, l. 76. Cf. p. 479, ll. 65–68; also p. 481, ll. 36–39.

[8] P. 478, l. 49; p. 479, ll. 18, 53.

[9] P. 481, l. 14, cf. ll. 36–39; p. 479, l. 53.

[10] P. 477, l. 45, cf. the whole passage ll. 39–52, also ll. 73–75; p. 486, ll. 12 sqq., especially from l. 37 to the end.

[11] P. 476, ll. 65–70; p. 481, l. 67–p. 482, l. 19, especially ll. 67, 68, 79–81 of p. 481.

this and other experiences she has suffered much,[1] but has a just and generous nature.[2] She is flattered and fawned upon by men whose reason for so doing, as she well knows,[3] is to secure their own advancement, — she with a nature starving[4] for real affection and hardening into marble[5] for the lack of it, but a nature of splendid intensity when set on fire.[6]

b. Norbert, the Prime-Minister[7] of the Kingdom — a position which he has held for one year — a man whose splendid statesmanship has done so much for the Queen during this year,[8] the greatest thing being that he has succeeded in combining two states and fixing the crowns of both on this Queen's head.[9] He is frank,[10] fearless,[11] and an ardent lover.[12]

c. Constance, the Queen's cousin,[13] young and beautiful,[14] taken to the Palace by the Queen[15] some time ago. Evidently Constance's parents are dead, although that is not stated. The Queen is Constance's guardian in fact, if

[1] P. 476, ll. 65–70; p. 478, ll. 49–52; p. 482, ll. 6–8.

[2] P. 476, ll. 14, 15, 35, 36; p. 478, ll. 45–94, especially ll. 48, 49, 56, 57, 65–69, 71–74, 79, 80; p. 480, ll. 41–72.

[3] P. 480, ll. 14–16, especially l. 16. Cf. also ll. 17 sqq.

[4] P. 478, l. 51.

[5] P. 480, ll. 4–36, especially ll. 7, 9, 21.

[6] See her whole conversation when she thinks Norbert loves her.

[7] P. 475, l. 51, cf. l. 52; cf. also p. 476, l. 27, and p. 480, ll. 4, 14, 15.

[8] P. 475, l. 53; p. 480, ll. 41–43; p. 485, l. 21.

[9] P. 475, ll. 53–59; p. 476, ll. 1–3.

[10] P. 478, ll. 2–9; p. 479, l. 10; and often. The "chaos of intrigues" in which he has been involved as Premier has been very distasteful to him (p. 478, ll. 10–22).

[11] P. 483, ll. 28, 29; and often. See also his whole attitude.

[12] P. 475, ll. 1–18; p. 477, l. 36; p. 478, ll. 10, 11; and very often.

[13] P. 476, ll. 13, 29; p. 477, l. 20; and often. Cf. p. 478, l. 72.

[14] P. 482, l. 22, cf. ll. 23–25.

[15] P. 478, ll. 71–74; p. 479, ll. 18, 19, 65; p. 481, ll. 21–24.

not in legal form. Constance is politic,[1] and not averse
to dissimulation.[2]

4. *The Occasion.*

The occasion is the great banquet[3] to celebrate the results
achieved by Norbert's statesmanship during the past
year. He is the centre of praise and congratulation.[4]
But he has slipped away from the festivities[5] for a moment,
even while the Queen is waiting for him to name his reward.[6]
As the poem opens, he stands here now in the balcony with
Constance.

5. *The Story.*

The story is very simple. Norbert has wrought so well
all the year, not for gain, not for honor, but for love of
Constance, the Queen's cousin. To-night in his hour of
triumph, his praise in every mouth, he feels sure he can
ask the Queen for whatever reward he will and it will be
granted. He begs Constance to let him tell the Queen his
love for her cousin and ask the Queen to grant him that
cousin's hand to-night. Constance insists that such a move
will disappoint the Queen, make her angry, and spoil

---

[1] See her argument in all the first four pages.   Contrast Norbert's replies.

[2] See her whole conduct in the last four pages of the poem, — her brazen
pretense, her effort to force Norbert to pretend that the Queen has understood correctly.

[3] P. 475, ll. 53, 54, 59.   Cf. p. 477, ll. 26–28; p. 478, ll. 13–16; p. 480,
ll. 41–43; p. 485, l. 21.   For a while I was accustomed to think there was a
council also this evening, in connection with the banquet.   This was on
account of p. 477, ll. 46–48, — supposing that Norbert had abruptly concluded this council and that the "one minute's meeting in the corridor"
was just now before the lovers came out on the balcony.   But undoubtedly
this is not so.   The council and the meeting in the corridor were at some other
time, in the year past, — one of the many secret interviews and communi-
cations of which others are mentioned in ll. 49–52, — all summed up in l. 53.

[4] P. 475, l. 59; p. 476, ll. 1–3.

[5] P. 477, ll. 41–44.

[6] P. 475, l. 7; p. 476, l. 4; p. 478, ll. 41, 42; p. 480, ll. 73–76.

the brilliant future which is open to Norbert in the government. Norbert declares that he doesn't want his love kept secret and insists upon telling the Queen now. Constance finally agrees, only insisting upon how he shall put the matter — she makes him promise to begin by flattering the Queen (contrary to Norbert's inclination), then to go on and tell her that Constance is as a ribbon the Queen wears, that Constance is so near the Queen that she seems a piece of the Queen's self, and that therefore he loves Constance, — so coming to the point and asking for Constance's hand. So Norbert goes in to ask.[1] He follows the method insisted upon by Constance — but unfortunately. Before he can get to the real point the Queen jumps to the conclusion that he is proposing *to her*. It is too good to be true, but she grasps his love and appropriates it, and rushes out on the balcony to find Constance and tell her about it. Poor Constance sees what has happened but cannot explain, and listens to the Queen going on about how beautiful and wonderful love is, how she will get free from the husband who has been tied to her but separated from her these many years, how much it all means in her life, and so on. The Queen goes back into the parlors, and Norbert comes again on the balcony to talk with Constance. In a few minutes the Queen comes out again. Constance makes a great "bluff," trying to force Norbert to act as if the Queen had understood aright. But Norbert, all frankness, will have none of it. The Queen sees her mistake and is overwhelmed with humiliation and anger, — that such hope should be awakened in her, only to turn at once to ashes. She goes in, and the heavy feet of the guard are heard coming to place Norbert and Constance under arrest.

[1] A brief interval (p. 479, between ll. 23 and 24), while Norbert speaks with the Queen.

The whole trouble has come through insincerity, or at least through the lack of frankness and directness. The Queen confesses to Constance that she thought Norbert was working for love and thought it was Constance he loved, and that she had decided to grant Constance's hand when he should ask it. Had he gone on as he wished this evening, all would have been well. Constance's wanting him to approach by flattery and to present his request in an indirect way made all the misunderstanding and disaster.

6. *The Excellence of the Poem.*

The excellence of the poem consists, then, not in its plot. That is slender and gives simply the ground for the dialogue. The excellence of the piece is the excellence of the conversation. It is a conversation almost altogether about love as the thing most worth while. Seldom will you find the matter put more passionately and beautifully. Norbert's declarations as to what love means are superior to those of either of the women. The Queen's are a close second, and Constance's a poor third. Perhaps no words of Norbert's are finer than those in which he defines his attitude toward life:[1]

> "I count life just the stuff
> To try the soul's strength on, educe the man."

If I were obliged to say which seems to me the most remarkable passage in the poem, I would say the passage in which the Queen describes her loneliness and heart-hunger in the midst of all their deference and adulation,[2] and especially the closing lines:[3]

> "There have been moments, if the sentinel
> Lowering his halbert to salute the queen,
> Had flung it[4] brutally and clasped my knees,
> I would have stooped and kissed him with my soul."

[1] P. 483, ll. 28, 29.
[2] P. 480, ll. 4-36.
[3] P. 480, ll. 33-36.
[4] *i.e.* had flung it down.

IX

A GROUP OF THE DRAMATIS PERSONÆ

WE have already discussed[1] a few of the shortest poems which appeared in *Dramatis Personæ*, 1864. We turn now to a group of the longer poems in that volume.

I. ABT VOGLER, pp. 499, 500

1. *Abt*, German, meaning *abbot*, — used here not in the sense of head of an abbey, or monastery, but in the sense in which the French word *abbé* is frequently used, *i.e.* as a title for an ecclesiastic who is not engaged in the regular Church work, but instead in literary, educational, or musical lines. For such a man we use in English *abbé*, instead of our own word *abbot*.

2. George Joseph Vogler was born in Würzburg, Bavaria, June 15, 1749. He was educated for the Church, and was ordained priest in Rome in 1773. He opened a school of music at Mannheim, in Baden, in 1775. About 1786 he went to Sweden, and founded a school of music in Stockholm. He invented an instrument called the *Orchestrion*, — a compact organ with four keyboards of five octaves each and a pedal board of 36 keys, the whole capable of being packed into small space for transportation. It is this instrument to which Browning refers.[2] With this instrument, Abbé Vogler travelled extensively and gave recitals, — often with meager success at first. His recitals in

---

[1] In Chapter V.

[2] In the words: "After he has been extemporizing upon the musical instrument of his invention," placed in parenthesis under the title.

London in January, 1790, were, however, received with great enthusiasm. Returning to the Continent, he now met with great success everywhere. He established his third school of music at Darmstadt, the capital of Hesse, in 1807, and there Weber and Meyerbeer were among his pupils. He died at Darmstadt, May 6, 1814.

Vogler was *Kapellmeister* (*i.e.* director of the band or orchestra, sometimes with a choir also, maintained at court) in Mannheim, Stockholm, and Darmstadt. He composed a number of operas (only the later ones proving in any degree successful) and some church music. His *Missa Pastoricia* (Pastoral Mass, Shepherds' Mass) is sung every Christmas at the Court-Chapel in Vienna.

3. Browning presents Vogler meditating over his keys, after extemporizing on his Orchestrion:

a. If he could only make music *visible*, then what he has been playing would appear as a palace. Then he goes on to describe that "palace of music."

b. Then he turns his thoughts upon the *creative power* which the musician has.

c. But the music which he created — which, if it could be seen as well as heard, would be a palace — is gone. Gone? No. Nothing good can die. All harmony exists unto eternity. This is the only thing that makes life worth while and gives it strong and victorious music —saves it from the minor key. It is "the C Major of this life."

4. Difficult points:

Stanza 1 — *as when Solomon willed*. Legends both Jewish and Mohammedan exalt Solomon's power and wisdom far beyond what is said of him in the Old Testament. The legends make him commander of the demons and of the powers of Nature. This power he owed to the fact that he possessed a seal with the ineffable name of the God

of the Hebrews on it.[1]   See the reference to this name later
in this stanza.   Cf. also stanza IX.

Stanza II — *nether springs*, lower springs, *i.e.* springs
at the bottom of the world.   The phrase is unfortunate
because men do not lay the foundations of a palace *on
springs*, nor on springy ground, but on rock.

Stanza III — *gold as transparent as glass*. Cf. Rev. 21 :
18, 21. *Outlining . . . Rome's dome*, the dome of St.
Peter's Church in Rome, which used to be, on great festivals
e.g. that of Easter, outlined by fixing on it thousands of
candles.

Stanza V — *Protoplast*, the thing first modelled, the
thing from which all the other similar things are copied.
The word is from the same root as the more familiar word
protoplasm, the physical basis of life, identical in the cells
of all living things.

Stanza VII — *that can, can* used as an independent verb,
not as an auxiliary, — used here as in "I can no more."
The will that can means the will that has power, the will that
does things, the will that creates.   *That out of three sounds
he frame, not a fourth sound, but a star — star* used figuratively, meaning something far above, far more striking
than, what we had before.   The point is: If you mix
three colors together, you will get a *color*.   But if you mix
three tones in a chord, the result will not be a fourth *tone*,
but a harmony of the three.   Thus the musician has a
sort of creative power.

Stanza XII — Vogler resumes now on his instrument,
beginning with a chord in the major key.   He modulates
into the minor key, and "blunts it into a ninth."   *Blunt*
here means to flat; *it*, the chord, or the note which de-

[1] We have given a brief discussion in regard to this name in Chapter II.
See p. 57.

termines the chord ; *a ninth* means an octave and one degree
additional, which in the major key amounts to an octave
and a full tone, but in the minor, in which Vogler is now
playing, amounts to an octave and a semitone over. A full
chord of the ninth consists of the root with its third, fifth,
seventh, and ninth. While playing in the minor, he "stands
on alien ground," because he has modulated away from the
major into music conveying a different impression, — the
major key expressing what is bright and exhilarating, the
music of hope, joy, victory, — the minor key being melancholy, the music of longing, discouragement, grief, despair.
He surveys "awhile the heights" (*heights* used figuratively
for the major from which he has gotten away), from which
he rolled "into the deep," *i.e.* into the minor key. "Which,
hark," — and as he suits the action to the word, we hear
him modulate back into the major key. *Which* is the
heights, the major; and he has "dared and done" the
heights when he has gotten back into the major key. The
point in "now I will try to sleep" is that life lived in C
Major is normal; in that a man may rest.

A detailed explanation of a modulation such as Browning
here describes is given by Miss Porter and Miss Clarke
in their note in the Camberwell Edition,[1] as follows:

Suppose Abt Vogler, when he "feels for the common chord,"
to have struck the chord of C major in its first inversion, *i.e.* the
third, E, in the bass, the fifth, G, at the top ; now, "sliding by semitones," that is, playing in succession chords with the upper note a
semitone lower, he would come to the chord A, E, C, which is the
(minor) tonic chord of the scale of A, the relative minor of C, and so
he would thus "*sink* to the minor." Now he blunts the fifth of this

[1] Camberwell Browning, vol. V, pp. 309, 310. We quote exactly, pre-
serving the punctuation. The same note verbatim will be found in the vol.
of Browning's *Poems* edited by the same ladies, 1896, pp. 476, 477, — its
earlier appearance.

chord E to E♭, which thus becomes a minor ninth over the root D, the whole chord being D, F♯, A, C, E♭, and, as he explains, he stands on alien ground because he has modulated away from the key of C, but, instead of following this dominant by its natural solution, its own tonic, which would be G, B, D, he treats it as if it were what is called a supertonic harmony. So, after pausing on this chord to survey awhile the heights he rolled from into the deep, he suddenly modulates back to C. He has dared and done, his resting-place is found — the C major of this life.

Miss Porter and Miss Clarke present [1] the music on the staff, to show the whole progression as described.

5. The best part of the poem is stanzas VIII–XII inclusive, the discussion of the persistence of all that is good — its survival beyond what is called death. This is at one with the faith Browning shows in so many poems, some of which we have already studied in this course.[2] Abt Vogler seems to go further than the other statements in declaring the survival of all that is good, beautiful, or harmonious. It is remarkable that Browning, with such positive faith as this, could nevertheless put himself so completely into the point of view of a man like Cleon and give expression so poignantly to the hunger for immortality and the despair of its being satisfied.

II. RABBI BEN EZRA, pp. 501–503

1. The man Rabbi Ben Ezra was a Jewish scholar and philosopher, born in Toledo, Spain, in 1092 A.D. His full name was Abraham ben Meir ben (or ibn) Ezra; he is usually cited as Aben Ezra or Ibn Ezra. He was always poor and studied hard. He travelled widely in Spain, France, Italy, Greece, and England. He gained fame as

---

[1] In both places referred to in our preceding note.

[2] e.g. *Prospice, Reverie,* and the *Epilogue* to *Asolando.* Cf. also, in *The Flight of the Duchess*, p. 363, ll. 98–100.

grammarian, theologian, astronomer, mathematician, poet, — but especially for his commentaries. In these commentaries, which are on most of the books of the Old Testament, he was one of the first of mediæval scholars to employ sound critical principles. He died in 1167. On his life and writings, the greatest work done in English has been done by Dr. M. Friedländer, whose studies include a translation of Ibn Ezra's *Commentary on Isaiah*, London, 1873,[1] and a series of *Essays on the Writings of Ibn Ezra*, London, 1877.[1]

2. Mr. A. J. Campbell declares that the distinctive features of Rabbi Ben Ezra's philosophy in Browning's poem are characteristic of the writings of the real Rabbi.[2] This shows Browning's way of doing. This poem is not a hit-or-miss piece of imagination. Browning informed himself in regard to Ibn Ezra's teaching (no doubt the poem was suggested by his reading in the writings of the Rabbi), and he gives here an epitome of how the real Ibn Ezra looked at life.

3. As to the *style* of Browning's poem :

While people are talking about Browning's taking so many words to say a thing, they should be reminded to read his *Rabbi Ben Ezra*, where the chief difficulties all arise from the *extreme condensation* — so few words expressing so much thought, in almost every stanza. Any stanza of the poem can be made plain by writing it out in full, *i.e.* supplying words and phrases implied. Indeed, this procedure is recommended. Take any stanza which you find difficult and try writing out the sentence completely in prose

---

[1] *Publications of the Society of Hebrew Literature.* Michael Friedländer, Ph.D., was for over 40 years (1865–1907) Principal of the Jewish College in London. He is the author of many works. See *Who's Who 1910*, p. 700.

[2] Campbell's notes on this point are given by Berdoe, *Browning Cyclopædia*, pp. 374–376.

form. You will be surprised to see how quickly it will straighten itself out.

4. As to the *philosophy*:

No poet in English has made old age so beautiful as Robert Browning has.[1] Old age is to Browning the fulfillment of youth and middle age, — the consummation of our earthly life.[2] He has set this forth in *Rabbi Ben Ezra* better than anywhere else.

a. Now growing old, looking backward over his life and forward to the great change which is called death, the Rabbi is serene and undismayed. Old age is the best of life, for which the earlier years were made; it is the fulfillment of God's plan.[3] Old age will only furnish him a chance to get perspective, to recognize what have been the real values in the past years, and to prepare himself to go forward into the unseen with the advantage gained from this review of his experience:[4]

> "And I shall thereupon
> Take rest, ere I be gone
> Once more on my adventure brave and new:
> Fearless and unperplexed,
> When I wage battle next,
> What weapons to select, what armour to indue."

b. With all the hardship and failure he has met, the Rabbi is glad that he chose high ideals, and would not accept anything else:[5]

> "What I aspired to be,
> And was not, comforts me:
> A brute I might have been, but would not sink i' the scale."

---

[1] Cf. the Gipsy in *The Flight of the Duchess*, p. 363, ll. 81–100.

[2] But cf. how keenly Browning puts himself in Cleon's place, p. 471, ll. 27 sqq.

[3] Stanza I.   [4] Stanza XIV.   [5] Stanza VII.

That is, the fact that he did struggle for what he could not attain shows what was in him, and is therefore a comfort to him. The struggle of the years will be found at last to have removed him forever from the plane of the developed brute; he will be the germ of a god:[1]

> "Thence shall I pass, approved
>   A man, for aye removed
> From the developed brute; a god though in the germ."

After all, what a man really has done is not to be estimated by the visible results on which the public can lay its hand and on which it can set a value:[2]

> "But all, the world's coarse thumb
>   And finger failed to plumb,
> So passed in making up the main account;
>   All instincts immature,
>   All purposes unsure,
> That weighed not as his work, yet swelled the man's amount:
>
>   Thoughts hardly to be packed
>   Into a narrow act,
> Fancies that broke through language and escaped;
>   All I could never be,
>   All, men ignored in me,
> This, I was worth to God, whose wheel the pitcher shaped."

c. No, man is not like a bird or beast, satisfied when filled with food. Man has something in him that will not be satisfied so.[3] Man is allied to the creative Power:[4]

> "Rejoice we are allied
>   To That which doth provide
> And not partake, effect and not receive!
>   A spark disturbs our clod;
>   Nearer we hold of God
> Who gives, than of His tribes that take, I must believe."

[1] Stanza XIII.
[2] Stanzas XXIII–XXV.
[3] Stanzas IV sqq.
[4] Stanza V.

The words "hold of" mean simply *are related to, partake of the nature of*. And because we partake of the nature of God, therefore hardships and sufferings are to be met with a high spirit:[1]

> "Then, welcome each rebuff
>   That turns earth's smoothness rough,
> Each sting that bids nor sit nor stand but go!
>   Be our joys three-parts pain!
>   Strive, and hold cheap the strain;
> Learn, nor account the pang; dare, never grudge the throe!"

d. The Rabbi does not believe in condemning the flesh and despising it as a clog to the spirit. We are not to say we have gained ground *in spite of* the flesh. Rightly understood, the body is good and the soul is good. In normal and complete living, the body will be up to its height and the soul up to its height, and each will help the other:[2]

> "As the bird wings and sings,
>   Let us cry 'All good things
> Are ours, nor soul helps flesh more, now, than flesh helps soul!'"

This is the answer to the question proposed in the latter half of stanza VIII.

e. The poem is permeated with irrepressible optimism and implicit faith in God. Death opens to us life's completion.[3] This earth is only a Potter's wheel on which God shapes us.[4] And the ultimate purpose of the cup (a human personality) so shaped is to do God service, beyond the gates of death. Browning, with the splendid audacity which so often characterizes his handling of a metaphor, presents a picture of the destination of the cup shaped on

---

[1] Stanza VI.   [2] Stanza XII.   [3] Stanza XXXII, last line.
[4] Cf. Is. 64:8; Jer. 18:1-6. This figure, in the prophets, of God as a Potter influenced St. Paul's thought also, Rom. 9:20 sqq.

purpose to bear wine to the lips of God [1] — the Rabbi says that never in the worst whirl of the earthly experience has he mistaken the end he will ultimately serve, viz. to slake God's thirst.[2]

5. The poem is compact of great thoughts, and it is quite unsatisfactory to try to summarize it. To read it, not merely once but scores of times, that is what makes its wholesome and invigorating views of life grow on a man. There is no poem of equal length which will do more to make a man calm and stern and glad than Browning's *Rabbi Ben Ezra*.

III. A Death in the Desert, pp. 503–512

1. The manner of presentation gives the work an air of antiquity which is very fascinating. This effect is produced by a statement in brackets, prefixed as if by an editor. The statement explains that what follows is from a manuscript supposed to be by Pamphylax, and describes the manuscript, its location in a particular chest, and its history. This last is really the master stroke: the editor has received the manuscript from Xanthus, his wife's uncle, now deceased. The impression received from this preface is increased by another explanation in brackets on the next page,[3] purporting to give a gloss originated by Theotypas. Something of a similar atmosphere is created by the matter enclosed in brackets at the end of the poem.

2. The poem purports to be an account of the death of the Apostle John.

a. The tradition of the Church from the latter half of the second century onward is that John came to an extreme age and was the last surviving of the Apostles. The tradition definitely associates the closing period of his life

---

[1] Stanzas xxix and xxx.   [2] Stanza xxxi.   [3] P. 504, ll. 33–55.

with the city of Ephesus in Asia Minor and places his death
in the time of Trajan, who became Emperor in the year
98 A.D.

b. Browning gives us here, from imagination, some sketch
of the circumstances under which John's death took place,
but that is not the main point. Whatever is said about his
death is only a frame for his last address, his dying message.
The circumstances related have a vivid reality except in
one point, and that is improbable: The dying Apostle is
unconscious, so far gone that it seems hardly possible to
rouse him at all; yet when he is finally roused, he sits up
and speaks page after page of keenly argued philosophy.
Of course, it is not physically impossible that the man's
vitality should thus reassert itself and give him an opportunity to spend all his last strength in this way, but it is
improbable. Apart from the question which arises on this
point, the setting which introduces the speech and follows it
is dramatic and picturesque to a remarkable degree.

3. The thing that stimulated Browning to write the argument which he here puts in St. John's mouth was the trend
of radical criticism, and especially Renan's *Vie de Jésus*
(*Life of Jesus*) published in June, 1863. That Renan's book
made considerable impression on Browning we see not
only here but in the *Epilogue* to the very volume in which
this poem appeared. In the *Epilogue*, the statement of
doubt and disappointment is put in the mouth of a "Second
Speaker, *as Renan.*" [1] In *A Death in the Desert* the chief
thing is Browning arguing against the extreme critical
position with which he had become acquainted. It is true
that Browning seems to be mixing up things pretty badly
when he puts an answer to nineteenth century criticism in
the mouth of St. John at the end of the first century. But

---

[1] P. 539, between ll. 75 and 76.